THE STAGE COMBAT HANDBOOK

A Tool for the Student of the Art of Stage Combat

WOLF CHRISTIAN...
...has been teaching stage combat since 1984. While living in London, he taught at RADA, Central, The Poor School, LISA, The City Lit, The Actor's Centre, The Royal College of Music and the Royal Academy of Music. He was a founder member of the British Academy of Stage & Screen Combat (BASSC), member of the Equity Fight Director's Register and served briefly on the Equity National Committee of Fight Directors.

With thirty years' experience as a stage combat instructor, fight director and actor under his belt, Wolf now teaches as a VT at the Arts University Bournemouth, specialising in Psychological Realism and Acting for Camera

Wolf lives by the sea with his wife, Mandi, and white German Shepherd, Calis.

Photograph: *Wolf Christian*
Image 2013 ©Jack Daniels 07831 356719

THE STAGE COMBAT HANDBOOK

By

Wolf Christian

A Tool for the Student of the Art of Stage Combat

Published by Wolf Christian 2014

Copyright © 2014 Wolf Christian
All rights reserved. This book or any portion thereof may not be reproduced or used in any manner whatsoever without the express written permission of the publisher except for the use of brief quotations in a book review or scholarly journal.

ISBN: 978-1-291-89516-2

www.wolfchristian.co.uk

DEDICATION

To my wife – she & I know why.
To my parents – they know why.
And to the memory of my sister – we all know why.

TABLE OF CONTENTS

The Stage Combat Handbook	i
Wolf Christian…	ii
Dedication	v
Table of Contents	vi
List of Illustrations	xiii
Acknowledgements	xiv
Principles of Stage Combat	1
Basic Stagecraft	4
Diagram 1 – A Rudimentary Compass	*6*
Diagram 2 – The Actor's Compass	*7*
Alignment	8
The Warm-Up	11
Footwork 1 – Advance & Retreat	27
All-purpose On Guard	27
On Guard Online	28
Diagram 3 – Finding the On Guard Foot Position	*31*
Adding the arms	31
Advance	35
Retreat	35
Diagram 4 – Footprints showing the Advance and the Retreat	*37*
Fingerwork 1 – Grip & Guards	38
Lines of Attack & Defence	40
Diagram 5 – Lines of Attack and Defence	*43*
Eight Guard Positions	44
The Sword	47
Diagram 6 – Parts of the Sword	*53*

How to Hold the Sword 53
The Extension 54
Finding Targets... 55
Footwork 2 - Lunge & Recover 58
The Lunge 58
Diagram 7 – The Lunge... *60*
Fingerwork 2 - Parries 62
The Path of the Parry 63
Unarmed 1 - Blocked Punch Exercise 66
Fingerwork 3 – Path of the Parry 73
The Path of the Parry (cont'd…) 73
Numbering the Parries 75
Low Line Parry Practice 80
High Line Parry Practice 83
Distance – Defining & Checking 87
Types of Fighting Distance 90
Checking Distance 91
Extending and Parrying (Again!) 93
Extend & Lunge, Parry, Recover 98
Cuts – Attacks With Edge 100
Making a Cut 100
Head Parries 103
The Path to Parry 5 104
The Path to Parry 5a 104
5 & 5a: Plenty of potential for hazard…..................................... 105
Head Cuts 106
Unarmed 2 – Reversal of Energy 108
Reversal of Energy 108

- Strangling 108
- Exercise: 109
- Hair Pull 115
- Transitions 118
  - Getting into the strangle 119
  - Show & Go 119
- Unarmed 3 - More Examples of RofE 122
  - Finger Squeeze 122
  - Interlocked Finger Wrestle 122
  - Nose Pull 123
  - Ear Pull 123
  - Testicle Grab 124
  - Nipple Tweak 124
  - Fishhook 125
  - Headlock 125
  - Arm Lock – Arrest 126
  - Arm Lock – Half Nelson 126
  - Strangle from Behind 127
  - Lifted Strangle Against a Wall 128
  - Ditto with Props 128
  - Leg Lock 128
  - Finger Lock 129
  - Rope Pull 129
  - Caveman Drag 129
  - Pulling & Pushing 130
- Unarmed 4 - Intro to Impact Moves 131
  - Elbow Attack to Stomach. 131
  - Stomach Punch 133

    The Box Masking Technique 136

    Knee to Stomach 136

    Kicking Technique 139

    Kick to Stomach 140

Rolls & Descents 143

    Forward Roll 144

    Shoulder Roll 146

    Curtsey Method Descent 148

    Big Step Descent 149

    Trip 150

    Backward Roll 152

    Backward Shoulder Roll 153

Unarmed 5 – Up & Down Slap 155

    Slapping 155

    The Up & Down Slap 157

Part Two 162

Footwork 3 – Pass Steps & More 163

    Pass Step 163

    Diagram 8 – The Pass Step Forward 167

    Lunge & Recover Forwards & Backwards 167

    Pass Lunge 170

    Then there is the Step Lunge. 170

    Reverse Lunge 170

Footwork 4 – Other On Guards 173

    On Guard Neutral 173

    On Guard Offline 175

    Diagram 9 – Four On Guard Foot Positions 179

Unarmed 6 - Taking a Knap 180

The Importance of Sound Effects 180
Knap - Definitions 181
Types of knap 183
Which Knaps Work When, Why & How 184
Footwork 5 – The Star & Compass 187
Avoidances 187
Ducking 189
Lateral Avoidances 190
Diagram 10 – The Fighter's Compass *192*
Star Footwork 193
Diagram 11 – Slips, Crosses and a Lunge *200*
Diagram 12 – Lunges and Slips *200*
Fingerwork 4 – Disengage & Coupé 201
Engage 201
Disengage 201
Coupé 202
Unarmed 7 - Cat Fighting 204
Foot Stamp – Up & Down 204
Foot Stamp – Profile 204
Foot Stamp – ITR 205
Bite – Your Lips 205
Bite – Your Thumb 206
Bite – Ever Widening 206
Eye Poke - Up & Down 206
Eye Poke – Profile 207
Scratch to Side of Face 208
Scratch to Front of Face 209
Fingerwork 5 – Counter Parries 210

Rolls & Descents 2 216
    Hands Free Roll 216
    Reaction Roll 216
    Dive Roll 217
Unarmed 8 - Punches 220
    Hook 220
    Jab (to the Face) 221
    Cross 222
    Uppercut 224
    Reverse Punch 226
    Hammerfist 227
Unarmed 9 - Blocked Punches 2 228
    Parrots & Ducks 228
    Blocking a Punch 228
    Ducking a Punch 231
Fingerwork 6 – Prise de Fer 234
    Taking the Iron 234
    Bind 234
    Croisé 234
    Envelop 235
    Bind Off! 236
    Parry 5 & 5a 237
    Beats 237
    Beat Parry 237
    Glissade 238
Unarmed 10 - Throws 239
    Hip Throw 239
    Irish Whip 240

    Stomach Throw 241

    Body Slam 243

Unarmed 11 – Profile & ITR Slaps 245

    Profile Slap 245

    Slap – In-The-Round 246

Unarmed 12 – Kicks to the Head 248

    Kneeling Kick to the Head 248

    Lying Kick to the Head 249

Unarmed 13 - Contact Punches & Kicks 252

    Flickhand Jab to Stomach 252

    Drag Flickhand 252

    Openhand to Stomach 252

    'Karate Chop' to Neck 253

    Double Fist to Back/Neck 253

    Foot Stomp to Stomach 256

    Repeated Stomps 258

    Walking Over the Stomach 258

    Contact Kick to the Stomach, Hands & Knees 259

Unarmed 14 – Head Butts & Smashes 260

    Head Butt, Up & Down 260

    Reverse Head Butt, Up & Down 261

    Head Butt, Profile 262

    Reverse Head Butt, Profile 263

    Standing Head Smash into Wall 265

    Head Smash on Floor/Table 266

    Headlock & Head Smash Into Wall 268

Rehearsal Notes 272

Index 277

List of Illustrations

Diagram 1 – A Rudimentary Compass
Diagram 2 – The Actor's Compass
Diagram 3 – Footwork: Finding the On Guard Foot Position
Diagram 4 – Footprints showing the Advance and the Retreat
Diagram 5 – Lines of Attack & Defence
Diagram 6 – Parts of the Sword
Diagram 7 – The Lunge
Diagram 8 – Footwork: The Pass Step Forward
Diagram 9 – Four On Guard Foot Positions
Diagram 10 – The Fighter's Compass
Diagram 11 – Slips, Crosses and a Lunge
Diagram 12 – Lunges and Slips
Photograph of the Author

Acknowledgements

My gratitude extends to all who have helped me in the study and practice of Stage Combat. Especially to William Hobbs, who introduced me to sword-fighting at drama school and whose lessons formed the foundations of my own; Terry King, who taught Physical Skills and Unarmed Combat and who showed me how to teach; and Richard Ryan who helped me to refine and develop my practice as we started the British Academy of Stage & Screen Combat (BASSC).

Fight Directors and Teachers from the old Society of British Fight Directors and the British Academy of Dramatic Combat (BADC) including Malcolm Ranson, Steve Wilshir, Nicholas Hall and Jonathan Howell, and Drew Fracher & Mark 'Rat' Guinn from the Society of American Fight Directors (SAFD), all of whom have unwittingly contributed to this book.

Concepts, guidelines, rules – all have been learned and/or stolen – have been adapted to suit the author, who only takes the credit – or the blame – for the writing. My thanks, too, to the many hundreds of students I have had the pleasure of teaching. I have learned from them at least as much as I have instilled.

Finally, an affectionate tribute to Henry Marshall, whose flamboyant and eccentric style as long-time Master-at-Arms at RADA provided entertainment and information in equal measure.

It is said of magic that anyone is welcome to practise the Art, providing they leave it the richer for their contribution. So it is with Stage Combat; please accept this book as my own very humble offering with which to enrich an Art which has given me such great pleasure.

Wolf Christian
Swanage
May 2014

Principles of Stage Combat

It is an illusion

The Art of Stage Combat – for Art it is – is one of illusion. It is deception. It is fraud. It is two parties convincing a third party (the audience) that they are seeing something they are not. It is, above all, not real. It is acting. It is 'Let's Pretend'. The acted intention must be real, as must be the acted emotions and feelings, the acted threat and danger, but the reality must be *safe*.

"**The safer a fight is for the actors to perform, the more dangerous the characters they are playing can make it appear.**" (Hobbs, 1983)

Think about that, for it is the fundamental principle which influences every element of this fine art.

Stage Combat cannot exist without a context

Done as exercises, the moves/tricks/gags that you will learn are only that – moves or tricks or gags. It is the same as a pirouette is only a move in ballet, or a coherent group of words is merely a sentence in a given language. But place those items within a dramatic context and those dry, albeit clever or nifty, little tricks contribute to a greater meaning capable of evincing powerful emotions – anger, joy, tears or laughter. But in exactly the same way that the lines need to be learnt before they can be given meaning, or the character has to be studied before it can be given life, so the techniques of stage combat have to become ingrained before the performer can fully utilise them. And that is repetitive, boring, sheer hard work. There are no short cuts. And none should be sought. The stakes are high: if you lie about learning the lines, you may dry and look stupid. If you lie about learning the fight properly, well... rather let it be illness and natural causes which drag the understudies from their knitting patterns and their crosswords...

Purpose of this manual...

...is not to *teach* you stage combat. The purpose of a book is to be read – either for enjoyment, information or reference purposes. This humble offering is intended as an accessory to a practical course. **You can only be *taught* by a stage combat teacher. You can be *informed* by any of a number of sources; but with a practical subject of this nature you must rehearse it in a suitable environment, under controlled conditions and with the supervision of a fully qualified and competent stage combat instructor.** Within these pages you will find many things in addition to technical instruction – comments, advice, Golden Rules, some rules which exist in the classroom at certain levels of study, but which are bent or broken in later stages - and an awful lot of the author's opinion. Take the book into the classroom and defile it. Question it. Vilify and ridicule it. Deface it and write your own notes or your own chapters. But use it. *(Especially in any class concerned with 'found weapons'!)* It is intended as a practical tool whilst you study, and as an aide memoire for the rest of your career.

Above all, this book is by no means definitive. Stage Combat is a living, breathing, developing beast and this – or any study of it – can only be a snapshot of one part of its development. If an idea in here has been improved upon and superseded then glorify that fact by recording it herein.

The order in which the subject matter here appears is an order which made sense to me for the purpose of writing. This is to say, it is not necessarily the order in which a teacher would teach it. Teachers will have their own valid reasons for how they teach their syllabus, and in what order, and this should be noted and acknowledged.

And finally in this chapter
Don't try to be smart. If you are starting - or are part way through - a stage combat course, refer to the relevant bits after you have been taught them. Do not try to second guess your teacher's syllabus, or to pre-empt it. Your teacher will have their own way of introducing and teaching techniques which will be more effective than reading them.

Disclaimer
The author cannot be held responsible for any accident arising out of unsupervised or irresponsible practice. This guide is intended as a workbook to be used alongside a stage combat course of instruction or as an aide memoire for anyone who has completed such a course.

Basic Stagecraft

Upstaging – location, location, location…

"Upstaging…" we have all heard of it. But what exactly is it? I have heard many definitions – 'doing better than them', 'stealing their thunder', 'taking the glory', etc. All correct definitions of what upstaging has come to mean in the vernacular, but where did the expression originate?

To understand this, you must have a rudimentary knowledge of stagecraft. Nothing scary, just 'knowing where the audience is', that sort of thing.

Imagine yourself standing on a conventional, proscenium-arch stage, (audience on one side, house tabs that can separate you from them and a picture-frame effect, from their point of view), facing the audience:

Now, as you take a step towards the front of the stage, nearer to the audience, you are moving downstage. Step backwards – away from the audience – and you are moving upstage. The third of the stage nearest the audience is Downstage, or DS. The third of the stage furthest from the audience is Upstage, or US. The band of stage in between is, amazingly, referred to as Centre Stage, CS. (Are you getting the conventions..?)

Move to your right as you face the audience (their left) and you are travelling Stage Right, SR. Go the other way, to

Basic Stagecraft

your left as you face the audience (their right), and you're heading Stage Left, SL.

The third of the stage to an actor's right – when facing the audience – is Stage Right, SR, and the third to the actor's left – when facing the audience – is Stage Left, SL. The third in-between is, wait for it…Centre Stage (CS)

In the old days directors had begun their life on stage as actors, graduating to standing in front of the actors to direct. So it was natural to speak the language of the actor and refer to left and right from the point of view of the many (the cast) instead of the one (the director). TV & Film directors tend not to have the same background, and therefore don't have quite the same sympathy with the actors as their theatrical counterparts, so directions to the actor from the director to move either left or right are, conventionally, Camera Left or Camera Right – i.e. from the point of view of the camera. Fair play, 'the many' usually comprise the *crew* on a TV or film set, so it is simply a case of bowing to mass appeal…

So we have a rudimentary compass: - Upstage or US: (furthest away from the audience), Downstage or DS: (nearest the audience) Stage Left or SL: the area to the actor's left as they look at the audience – as opposed to the onstage area to the left as viewed by the audience, which is Stage Right (or SR).

Basic Stagecraft

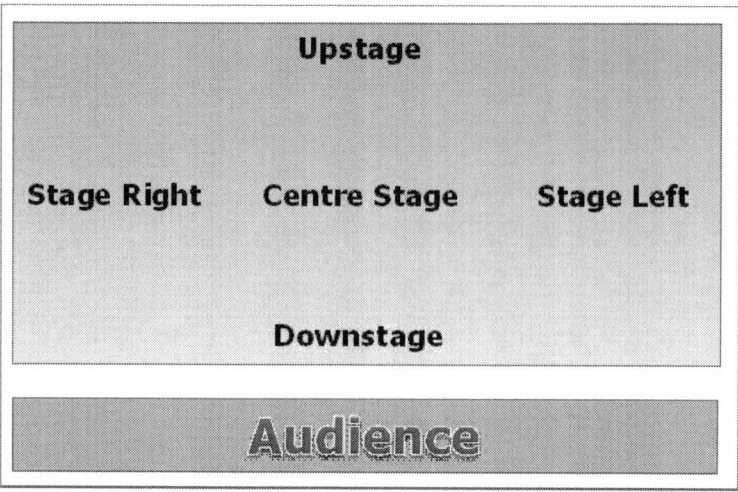

Diagram 1 – A Rudimentary Compass

But what of the corners? They look a little bare!
Exercise 1 – add these points to the compass:
Down Stage Left (DSL)
Down Stage Right (DSR)
Up Stage Left (USL)
Up Stage Right (USR)
Thus it is that all movement on a stage is directed, interpreted and recorded in these universal terms – an actor's compass.

Basic Stagecraft

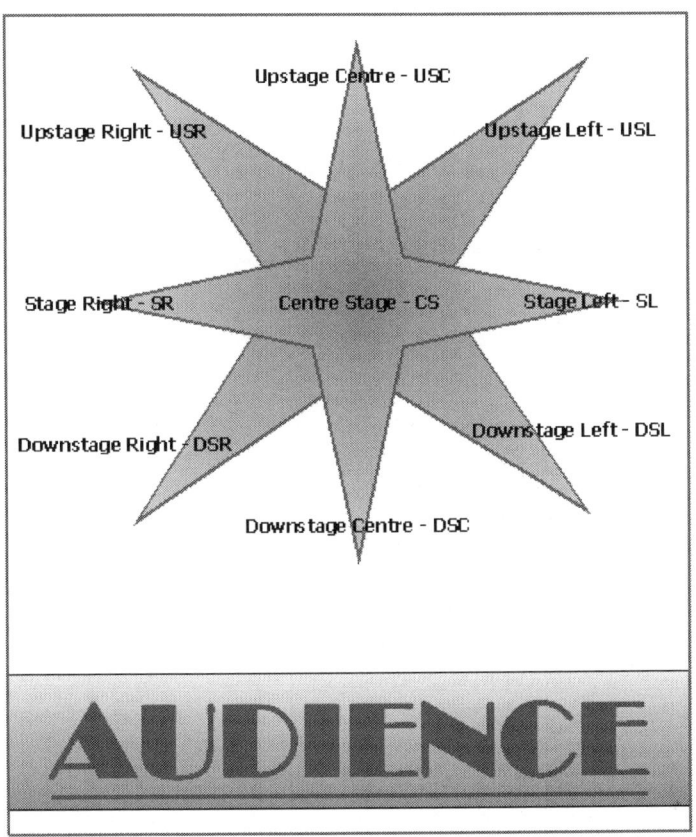

Diagram 2 – The Actor's Compass

SL is also referred to as Prompt Side (PS) as the wings on that side usually accommodate the desk and Deputy Stage Manager to run the show; SR is also OP – Opposite Prompt. (And a desk/DSM located on that side is referred to, affectionately, as a Bastard Prompt.)

This can get confusing when the actor relocates to a film set: there is no legacy theatre tradition of director coming from the boards; rather, the director and camera crew traditionally only see things from their side, so if asked by the director to move a little to the right, the actor must move to their LEFT (if they are looking directly at the camera). Or stage left (SL) in theatrespeak. Because the director is referring to *camera* right – towards the right edge of the frame as viewed through the lens.

Directions can confuse actors; this is why we are driven to locations by taxi...

Alignment

Alignment refers to the actors' on stage geographical relationship as perceived by the audience. Assume, for now, that we are working on a proscenium arch (picture frame) stage, with the audience on one side (the front).

Up & Down – one actor is standing immediately downstage of the other (who is, *ipso facto*, standing directly upstage of them). An unnatural placement for actors because of the upstaging and masking problems, but the most forgiving set-up for a lot of basic stage combat techniques.

Profile – the actors are facing each other, each at right angles to the audience, exposing one side of their faces, their profile, to the groundlings.

A technique may be described as 'up & down' or 'profile': this refers to the position of the actors in relation to the audience. Alignment is usually employed to hide something from the audience. And that which is hidden is referred to as 'the cheat'.

Safety First

At every level safety is paramount. Stage combat within these pages is aimed specifically at actors who wish to perform the techniques within a dramatic context - and then get on with the rest of the play, and the run.

Safety precautions and techniques - usually called 'safeties' - have to be built in from the first, and then drilled until the performer applies them instinctively. This involves hard work, concentration and repetition.

A large part of the Handbook will be reiterating and stressing the safeties which must be inherent within the moves. Remember the wise word of William Hobbs: "The safer a fight is for the actors to do, the more dangerous the characters can make it appear."

Basic Stagecraft

So how?

1. Eye-contact - The first, last and intermediate safety. The eyes have it. Entire paragraphs can be conveyed in a single glance, from "Don't worry; I've got you" to "Drat! I'm a little bit lost and appear to have forgotten the next move".
2. Rehearsal - Practice makes perfect…
3. Understanding - If you don't understand something, ask. Don't just 'give it a go' in the hope that it might be right.

Thought for the Day "I don't want to hurt myself or anyone else, nor do I want to get hurt by them."

The Warm-Up

Introduction to the Warm-Up

Before commencing any physical activity it is essential to warm up the muscles and joints to help prevent injury. Warm-ups are not exercise: they are *preparation* for exercise. They are deeply personal affairs and should not be seen as a competition in which you attempt to stretch further then the next person. Your warm-up should also reflect the work you are about to undertake – some exercises will be more specific to certain parts of the body than others, so ensure you prepare the relevant bits. Finally, and most important contextually, Stage Combat is performed by actors, therefore the warm-up should also reflect the other disciplines in which the actor is trained and used as a way of complementing that training, not detracting or opposing it. The most obvious example of this is the voice. All the time, effort and money invested in training in the optimum breathing and relaxation techniques to maximise your vocal potential counts for nothing if, the instant you draw your sword or square up to the villain, every muscle contracts and your throat constricts. The strangulated squeaks and high-pitched grunts that betray a tense vocal system will cause damage which short-term may result in you being 'off' for the next performance or even – long-term – may require surgery to repair.

On top of all the moves, tricks and techniques that you will learn and execute, it is paramount to learn them from day

The Warm-Up

one in a manner conducive to safe and effective voice production.

And one of the simplest ways to be aware of what the subcutaneous body is doing is to ensure that you are *breathing*. It is amazingly commonplace that, many times during the course of an average day, people forget to breathe…even when sitting down and doing nothing more taxing than staring out of a window, lost in thought, it is not unusual to unwittingly hold your breath. So force yourself to always be conscious of your breathing – if you are relaxed enough to breathe professionally than your whole body will be in a relaxed and tension-free state to perform physically to greatest effect, with minimum effort and significantly lower risk of injury.

Start with the first stretch (below) and see how easy it is to hold your breath! To start with you will have to force yourself to breathe evenly and continuously and correctly until, at some future point, your body has learnt to do this move and breathe at the same time. (See note on *'physical memory'*).

The Warm-Up

1 – Simple Stretch, Roll Down & Rebuild

i.   Stand with feet flat and about hip width apart, weight equally distributed;

ii.   Gently start to extend your arms vertically with the fingers reaching towards the ceiling (the sense should be that you are being led gently by the fingertips, and the arms follow until they are 'pulled' straight and vertical);

iii.   Check that you are breathing…

iv.   Now allow the fingers of one hand to be pulled a little more than the other so that you feel a gentle stretching down one side of your body;

v.   Relax the first hand and allow the other hand to reach a little further, transferring the vertical stretch across your back until it runs down the opposite side;

vi.   Repeat 1.iv; then repeat 1.v; always monitoring the breathing;

vii.   Now allow yourself to be pulled upwards by both sets of fingertips so that your heels lift a centimetre or two from the ground. Hold for a moment (check breathing!), and, with a sense of leaving the head exactly where it is, slowly lower the heels until the feet are flat;

viii.   Allow the fingers to relax and droop, then the hands, and then relax the elbows as the arms lower towards the floor. As the hands gently come past the face allow the neck and head to relax, then the shoulders. With a sense that each vertebra is gently sliding forwards and down off the shoulders of the one below, gently relax down through the spine. Flex the knees as you go down the spine so as not to 'pull' at any muscle at the back of the

The Warm-Up

legs. You should finish bent double with your fingers dangling downwards (if your eyes are open you will be looking backwards through your legs). Take a moment to concentrate on the breathing, making sure that it is relaxed and even, and not having to be pushed or forced.

ix.   Wiggle your hips from side to side and try to send a sideways ripple down your spine and along your arms to your fingers. Gently rock the hips forwards and backwards and try to send a vertical ripple along the same path;

x.   When you have mentally gone through each part of your body to see how relaxed it is, and ensured that you are indeed still breathing, then gently reverse the process in 1.viii, building upwards through the spine, leaving the head as the last thing to bring you back to fully upright. And breathe!

2 – Heel Lifts

i.   With the feet hip width apart, slowly lift up onto the balls of the feet as high as you can without allowing the ankles to drift out and the weight to transfer to the outside of the little toe. To prevent this think of pushing the ankles together, or even rolling inwards a little towards the big toes; (*Positive Negativity*: Rather than not doing something by thinking "I mustn't do that", or simply being given the negative instruction: "Don't do that", which creates a negative emphasis, usually to the detriment of the piece of work you are trying to achieve, focus on something positive. Therefore, instead of thinking "I must stop my ankles rolling out" - which turns the affair into an exercise

The Warm-Up

about NOT doing something - think "Can I push my ankles *in* a little while I do this"; this leads to a positive outcome and a measurable sense of achievement. Not merely "Yes! I *didn't* do it!")

ii.   Lower the heels back to the ground. The whole exercise, simple as it is, must be focused on being performed with the foot and lower leg remaining in the same line, i.e. someone watching from the front – or you checking yourself in the mirror – would only see vertical and not horizontal movement. (*Glass Walls*: Sometimes it is helpful to imagine that you are working with a glass wall, or walls, and/or ceilings. In this case, two small glass walls would be erected either side of each ankle, parallel with the feet. The emphasis, obviously, is not to break the glass with a sideways move at the ankle. Again, Positive Negativity in that: "Yes! I didn't smash the glass!" is the preferred outcome to "Ooops! I succeeded in smashing the glass".)

iii.   Give both feet a little shake (alternately!). The 'little shake' is useful after each stretch as it injects a bit of dynamic 'life' into the specific body part, whilst also dissipating any tensions which might have crept in to parts of the body while your attention was elsewhere. Also, it reminds you to breathe…

The Warm-Up

3 – Ankle Flex

i. Starting with the feet hip width, shift all the weight to one foot to enable you to raise the heel of the other about ten centimetres from the floor, the toes pointing upwards at about 45°;

ii. Now point the toes away from you, towards the floor. Think of pointing, specifically, the big toe. This will help to prevent 'sickle foot', that is, the leg straight and the foot twisting inwards at the ankle. Next, flex the foot so that the big toe is trying to look back up along the front of the leg. The muscles down the front of the leg should feel tight and the back of the lower leg should feel a little stretched; (*Muscle Pairs*: Roughly speaking, muscles work in pairs in opposition to each other. For example, hold your arm out straight in front of you, palm up. To bend the arm and bring the hand towards your face you have to contract the bicep. The shortening/contraction of this muscle is balanced by a corresponding lengthening/stretching of the muscle along the back of the arm, the triceps. During the course of this warm-up there is a conscious effort to work one muscle and then its opposite number. Sometimes, of course, there are muscle groups.)

iii. Repeat 3.ii & 3.iii approximately ten times then give the foot a little shake.

The Warm-Up

4 – Ankle Circles

i.   From position 3.i, fully flex the foot: rotate it, so that the toes describe as big a circle as possible, before returning to the flexed position. Do this about five or six times;

ii.   Repeat the exercise, rotating the foot in the opposite direction, and give the foot a little shake;

iii.   Change feet and repeat 4.i & 4.ii with the other foot.

5 – Knee Flex and Rear Thigh Stretch

i.   Stand with feet together, legs straight, and bend your trunk forward to allow you to place a hand on each knee;

ii.   Flex the knees over the toes as far as possible without allowing the heels to lift. (The thought should be to push the knees into the hands). Hold for a moment;

iii.   Push the hands into the knees and allow the legs to return to straight. Lean forwards a little and think of the muscles at the back of the upper leg relaxing, in order that they may lengthen. (As opposed to thinking of 'stretching' the muscles). Exhaling as you do this allows the muscles to relax a little more and consequently will lengthen further. On no account 'bounce' in this position: the ensuing 'burn' that you will experience is muscle tissue tearing and is not desirable here; (In the past it was popular to "Work 'til you burn" or aspire to "Feel the burn". Muscle tissue

The Warm-Up

regenerates very quickly and there is indeed a process of working-out muscles and stressing them to the point of tearing - the "burn" - in order that they repair bigger and stronger or longer and stronger. This is 'exercise' not 'warm-up' and it has a place in sport and/or vanity but not so much in stage combat.) Hold for a moment;

iv.   Repeat ii & iii about six times, then give the legs a little shake. This helps to warm up the knee joint more than muscles, and also the Achilles tendon. It is easy to forget about bones, cartilage, tendons and ligaments etc. and only remember to warm up muscles. (*Synovial Fluid*: the body's natural lubricant for the joints is synovial fluid. Its presence allows the bones and cartilage of the joints to move against each other smoothly reducing wear and tear, exactly like the oil in car's engine keeps the parts moving without seizing. And just like an engine, the parts need to move to get the juices flowing.)

6 – Buttock and Front Thigh Stretch

i.   Standing, shift the weight to one foot and bring the other knee up in front of you flexed and relaxed. Clasp the top of your shin just below the knee. (Do this with overlaid, not interlocked fingers – if you lose balance interlocked fingers can lock together, exacerbating the situation. (*Balancing*: balance is vital in Stage Combat. Balancing on one leg is worthwhile practice. A couple of tips for the beginner: 1-eyeline: focus on something in front of you at eye level; 2-mass: slightly flex the supporting leg which will lower your centre of gravity);

The Warm-Up

ii.	Gently squeeze the knee into your chest, hold for a moment, and then relax the squeeze. Repeat this 'squeeze & ease' about six times;

iii.	Release the knee, lower the leg and bend it backwards to bring the heel up towards your buttock. Grasp the instep with both hands and gently pull the sole of your foot more tightly in towards your buttock, hold for a moment, then relax. Repeat about six times. And shake.

iv.	Repeat 6.i – 6.iii with the other leg. (It is possible, and acceptable, to do this stretch with one hand, especially if you require the other to lean on a wall or partner's shoulder for support. In this case, ensure that you use the opposite hand – right foot, left hand; left foot, right hand. Using the same hand can pull the foot sideways, alongside your upper leg, putting unwanted and possibly damaging diagonal stresses on the knee.)

7 – Inner Thigh Stretch

i.	Spread feet as far apart as is comfortable;

ii.	Transfer the weight over to the left leg, flexing the left knee to a right angle and keeping the right leg straight, as you do this allow the toes of the right foot to lift off the ground and point to the sky. The stretch should be felt along the inside of the right thigh;

iii.	Transfer the weight across to the right leg. Repeat six times. And shake. (For extra stretch, as the toes lift and point up, allow the supporting knee to flex further, to an acute angle, trying to get the buttock as close to the corresponding heel as possible.)

The Warm-Up

8 - Hopping
i.   Hop on left foot whilst shaking out the entire collection of muscles and joints in the right leg;
ii.   Repeat on the right foot.

9 – Hand Shakes
i.   Feet shoulder width;
ii.   Bend elbows;
iii.   Shake hands out from the wrist, up and down, and then side to side.

10 – Arm Rotations
i.   Feet shoulder width;
ii.   Step forward with left leg;
iii.   Lightly clench right fist;
iv.   Circle the straight arm from the shoulder – front, up, back, down, not out to the side or across in front of you;
v.   Accelerate the circles until you feel a tingle in the fingers/hand;
vi.   Stop and shake the hand;
vii.   Change feet and repeat with the other arm.

11 – Wrist Stretch
i.   Feet shoulder width;
ii.   Bend the right elbow, raising the forearm to vertical in front of you, the thumb pointing directly at your nose. Relax the hand and allow it to droop forward (to create a floppy 'mime-ventriloquist' hand);

iii.   With the left hand, place the thumb on the edge of the wrist nearest you and the forefinger on the edge that is furthest away, to the forearm side of the joint. This will allow you to rest the heel of the left hand on the *back* of the right, not on the fingers;

iv.   By gently pushing down on the right hand with the left, lightly over-stretch the right wrist joint (you will feel a stretch on the outside (top) of the joint and a compression on the inside);

v.   Release the wrist;

vi.   Repeat four times;

vii.   Straighten and extend the right arm to the front and down;

viii.   Place the fingers of the left hand across the palm of the right and the left thumb across the back of the right hand just to the hand side of the wrist joint (to hold the right hand in your left 'vent' hand);

ix.   Gently pull the right hand backwards to stretch the inside of the wrist and compress the outside;

x.   Relax the stretch;

xi.   Repeat four times;

xii.   Shake out the hand/wrist;

xiii.   Repeat all with the other side.

12 – Shoulder Circles

i.   Feet shoulder width, arms dangling loosely at your sides;

ii.   Isolating and rotate the shoulders slowly, to their maximum extent, forwards;

The Warm-Up

iii.   Complete ten rotations;

iv.   Rotate backwards ten times. (While you are doing this, take turns at shaking the arms from the elbows to ensure their relaxed state and similarly move the head to ensure that the neck is free).

13 – Head and Neck

i.   Feet shoulder width;

ii.   Starting from the head at a neutral, centred, relaxed position floating at the top of the spine;

iii.   Turn the head to look left;

iv.   Return to centre;

v.   Turn the head to look right;

vi.   Return to centre;

vii.   Drop the chin onto the chest to look down;

viii.   Return to centre;

ix.   Raise the chin to tilt the head backwards to look up – slacken the jaw and allow the mouth to open to help ensure no tension;

x.   Return to centre;

xi.   Tilt the head sideways to the left as if trying to place the left ear onto the left shoulder – ensure that you do not raise the shoulder to meet the ear;

xii.   Return to centre;

xiii.   Tilt to the right;

xiv.   Return to centre;

xv.   Repeat 11.i – 11.xiv six times, taking care to return to centre between each move.

The Warm-Up

14 – Torso Twist

i. Stand with feet shoulder width apart;

ii. Hold left wrist with right hand, arms in front of your chest, as if around a tree (or beer keg…). Now rotate at the waist to the right, leading from the shoulders. Do not allow the hips to turn. Hold the stretch for a count of four;

iii. Pass through the start position and rotate trunk the other way and hold – ensure that the hips do not move;

iv. Repeat three times.

15 – Side Stretch

i. Stand with feet shoulder width apart;

ii. Slide left hand down left leg as far as you can without allowing the body to twist in any way (as if sandwiched front and back between two sheets of glass);

iii. Allow the right arm to bow, ballerina-like, above your head, so that you can look up into the palm of that hand. (For extra stretch, rotate the hand away from you so that the palm faces the sky and you are looking at the back of the hand.);

iv. Hold for a count of four;

v. Come back up through standing and repeat on the other side;

vi. Repeat four times.

The Warm-Up

16 – Back Stretch

i.   Feet a little more than shoulder width;

ii.   Place the hands on the lower back at either side of the spine (either the palms or the fists, experiment to see which gives the most support);

iii. Leading from the top of the head, slowly arch backwards – let the eyes lead, looking up the opposite wall to the ceiling, along the ceiling and down the wall behind you. If you can see the floor and start to follow it along towards your heels, fantastic!);

iv. Hold the stretch for a slow count of four, whilst making sure that you are breathing…!;

v.   Slowly come back to upright reversing the journey, that is, building from the base of the spine up;

vi. When you are fully upright, drop the chin onto the chest and, with a sense that each vertebra is gently sliding forwards and down off the shoulders of the one below, and gently relax down through the spine. Flex the knees as you go so as not to 'pull' at any muscle at the back of the legs. You should finish bent double with your fingers dangling downwards (if your eyes are open you will be looking backwards through your legs). Take a moment to concentrate on the breathing, making sure that it is relaxed and even, and not having to be pushed or forced.

vii. Wiggle your hips from side to side and try to send a sideways ripple down your spine and along your arms to

The Warm-Up

your fingers. Gently rock the hips forwards and backwards and try to send a vertical ripple along the same path;

viii.   When you have mentally gone through each part of your body to see how relaxed it is, and ensured that you are indeed still breathing, and then gently reverse the process, building upwards through the spine, leaving the head as the last thing to bring you back to fully upright. And breathe!

This is a gentle, general warm-up designed for actors and drama students to prepare for a class in stage combat. It takes into consideration many things, not least the movements they are likely to encounter, and their physical expectations – not those of a world-class athlete, perhaps, but still significantly higher than those of people in less physical occupations. Having said that, the warm-up is an adaptable beast from the point of view that you may wish to concentrate more on certain elements than others if the particular class content will be more specific to certain areas than others. Of course, if you are a trained dancer for example – or indeed a world-class athlete in whatever field – then you will have an awareness of warm-up exercises/routines which may work better for you.

The one constant, however, is that you *must* warm up your body (and voice) before engaging in any physical exercise.

The Warm-Up

Warm-Down

Equally important – and frequently overlooked – is the need to warm down after exercise. As well as letting your body know that the exercise part is over, it helps to dispel the build-up of lactic acid in the muscles which can cause cramping. Gently marking through the warm-up at a much reduced intensity can constitute your warm-down, or even a few minutes walking around the perimeter of the studio or hall you have been working in, whilst shaking out the extremities and checking the body for tensions, can suffice.

It is your body – your tool and your fortune – take care of it.

Footwork 1 – Advance & Retreat

All-purpose On Guard

You cannot build a house without foundations, so you cannot fight safely without sound footwork. Without it you will be off-balance and a danger to yourself and others around you. You therefore, cannot possibly spend too much time learning and revising footwork so that, when your mind is focused on acting, your feet will be in automatic.

Stand up: you are ready for moving.

On Guard; you are ready for fighting…

And there are many, many different on guard positions depending on things like the weapon of choice and hand of the combatant.

So let us begin with the most demanding; the on guard position, and basic footwork, of modern fencing.

Martial Arts grow and develop as man goes through evolution. Modern fencing is a distillation and refinement of centuries of swordplay – a never-ceasing quest for the most efficient, fastest and devious method of landing the hit. Once these techniques are learnt, it is relatively simple to undo the ages and step back in time to learn the less sophisticated footwork associated with the more rudimentary weapon systems.

Footwork 1 – Advance & Retreat

On Guard Online

Standing square to an opponent merely presents them with the biggest possible target. Standing side on gives them the narrowest. And leading with the side that presents the weapon makes the most sense...

Since Roman times left-handed people have been looked upon with suspicion by the majority, right-handed population ('left' = 'sinister' in Latin, 'right' = 'dexter'). And you were taught to sword fight right-handed regardless. We live in more enlightened times, and realise that some people are more comfortable using their sinister side. And if they have more control using their left than their right, it makes sense that they should be allowed to use their more controlled side in the interests of safety.

So here, there is no right or left; merely 'sword side' and 'non-sword side'. Sword side refers the side of the body corresponding to the arm that is attached to the hand which grips the weapon most readily in combat. Not the side of the body where the weapon rests in its scabbard...

To begin, stand upright at right angles to the direction of your (at this stage, imagined) adversary. Your sword arm will be nearest to them, your toes will be pointing at ninety degrees away from them.

Turn your sword foot *('sword foot' – the foot corresponding to the side which bears the sword, so for example a right-handed sword-wielder has a right sword foot; their right leg is their 'sword leg', right*

Footwork 1 – Advance & Retreat

side their sword side etc.) and point your little swordy toes at your opponent. Your feet will be heel to heel, at right angles to each other: your body will have pivoted a little to be at a comfortable forty-five degrees. You will have to work against this to force your body to remain at right angles to your foe to present the smallest possible target area, your sword side. To further complicate this, and to add to your discomfort, your head will be at ninety degrees to your body, fully-facing your foe. So nose and sword side toes are foe-facing, non-sword side toes and torso are side-on.

From here, take a step forward with your swordy, foe-facing foot, so your heels are hip-width apart. The heel of the non-sword foot is on a line with your sword heel and the ball of your sword foot, a line which, in time, will form an imaginary tightrope which will pass under the swordy ball, heel and non-sword heel of your opponent's foot.

Use a crack between the floorboards, a join in the carpet, or draw a line with chalk, or lay a line down with PVC insulation tape. Line is vital. Start with a physical one until a virtual one has become ingrained in your physical memory. *("Physical memory" – a movement or stance or sequence of moves can be repeated often enough that they become stored within your muscles and can become the default settings for your body. It is generally easier to write a programme from new then to alter a similar, incorrectly or badly learned one.)*

Footwork 1 – Advance & Retreat

Now bend the knees until the patellae are directly over the toes. Imagine that your spine, like a stick or rod, extends down into a groove in the middle of your line on the floor. This spine, or stick, is of a fixed length which does not allow you to bob up or down, but keeps your body at the same distance from the floor as you stand on guard and move backwards and forwards along your line.

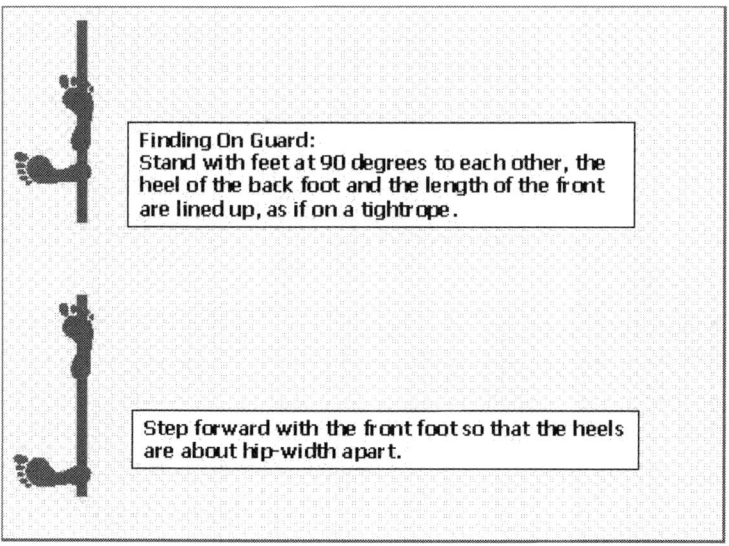

Diagram 3 – Finding the On Guard Foot Position

Adding the arms

In a short time you will be moving - Advancing, Retreating, Passing and Recovering - with a sword in your hand, so let us put the arms in place:

Footwork 1 – Advance & Retreat

Dangle your sword arm at your side; now raise the forearm so that it is parallel to the ground and point the forefinger, as a mini-sword, at your imaginary opponent's navel. Your sword hand can rotate through 180 degrees quite comfortably: with the forefinger straight and the other fingers curled, supinate the hand so that the palm faces the ceiling. Now pronate the hand – that is, rotate it so that the back of the hand now faces the ceiling and the palm faces the floor. Supination is the position of choice. Pronation is a good second. Half way between, with the thumb nearest the ceiling and the outside of the little finger facing the floor is a third position generally only used when cutting down into someone's skull, or to demonstrate an ignorance of sword training as a character choice.

Now clench the non-sword hand into a fist and place it between your sword elbow and your body, thumb touching your body. This is the distance your sword arm should be from your body in the on guard position.

So, you are on guard, feet hip width apart and at ninety degrees to each other, knees bent with the kneecaps over the toes, weight evenly distributed, your sword arm elbow a fist's width out from your body and your sword hand pronated so you are looking down at the back of your hand. Now straighten and raise your non-sword arm comfortably behind you with the hand a little higher than your head and the palm facing the sky.

Footwork 1 – Advance & Retreat

You should now be feeling a little like Errol Flynn or Douglas Fairbanks…

You are now ready to use the 'advance' and 'retreat' footwork to move this heroic on guard position along the line. You must imagine an opponent opposite you, on the same line, moving backwards and forwards with you.

As with all work, do this slowly and meticulously, going through all the checkpoints of the positions and motions, and be hard on yourself; when you have a real person opposite you and you are both whirling weapons - and having to act - the last thing you will want to think about is what your feet are doing.

Moving forwards & backwards

To move forward and backwards – or towards and away from your opponent – requires several criteria to be met:

Efficient – no extraneous movement which will take up time and energy;

Swift – while you need to be able to move rapidly in (forwards) to make an attack, you will want to be even quicker going out (backwards) to avoid the counterattack;

Safe – you will want to remain balanced and completely in control of your position at all times, positive yet not over-committed.

Footwork 1 – Advance & Retreat

We are in an on guard position carefully selected and honed for its suitability to fighting with a single sword: we will not change the body/arm positions while moving, as this would make us more vulnerable for the reasons mentioned in the section about on guards. The impression and thought should be of a sculpture of a perfect on guard being wheeled smoothly backwards and forwards.

To achieve all this takes time and effort to learn; you will also need to be aware of the compromises that are made to achieve our aims. To retain balance, to keep our feet on the floor for the maximum time (i.e. to be on one foot for the *minimum* amount of time) we keep the movements short, with the feet moving the least possible distance through the air, to achieve a significant result – the steps are small.

The body from the knees up remains in position, neither bobbing (up and down) nor swaying (side to side or backwards and forwards) – this retains the balance by keeping the centre of gravity low and as close to 50/50 over the feet at all times. Bobbing takes unnecessary effort of the legs and adds time to the steps, swaying plays havoc with the balance. Essentially, the feet do the moving and the body follows, as if on wheels. Too large a step with the front foot while advancing leaves all the weight on the back foot and requires almost total weight shift from one to another. Not only does this take time, but once you have shifted all your weight to the front foot to bring the

Footwork 1 – Advance & Retreat

back foot up you are unable to retreat until you can shift all your weight backwards again, having to overcome a mass of inertia. Allowing the back foot to creep up to the front foot results in you standing on guard on one spot, which has balance implications. So to retain balance, posture and safety while moving in the swiftest and most efficient manner we take a small, precise step, with the leading foot to start the move, and close it with a precise step of the same length with the trailing foot.

Advance

1. Raise the swordy toes and quickly move the swordy heel onto the spot on your line vacated by the toes. (At this point you can still recover – that is, go back to your original on guard position – you have not yet committed to moving forward.) Having decided to follow through with the advance, do the next three things in order, as three separate parts of what will become one movement:
2. Place the swordy ball down on the floor;
3. Place the non-sword ball one foot-length forward, parallel to your line, on the floor;
4. Put down your non-sword heel.

Slowly practice the four elements of the advance so that step 1 corresponds to the first syllable – 'ad' – and steps 3, 4 & 5 happen in order, on the second syllable – 'vance'. So, on the word 'ad', step forward onto the sword heel;

Footwork 1 – Advance & Retreat

On the word 'vance' place the sword toes, then the non-sword toes and finally the non–sword heel in a musical triplet.

Retreat

The almost-exact reverse of the advance:

1. non-sword ball leads
2. non-sword heel is placed
3. sword ball
4. sword heel.

Step 1 happens on 're-', steps 2, 3 & 4, in order, happen on '-treat'.

Note that these are small steps which glide the on guard position up and down your line by the length of one of your feet. The time when the weight is *not* 50-50 over your feet is kept to a minimum.

Working with a partner, have them call out either "advance" or "retreat", and see if you can follow their instructions. And whether they can manoeuvre you back to your start position. Mark your start position with a chalk or tape line behind your back foot and see how good you are. For example, do three advances followed by three retreats, in any combination, land you back on the exact start spot? Practice until it does.

Footwork 1 – Advance & Retreat

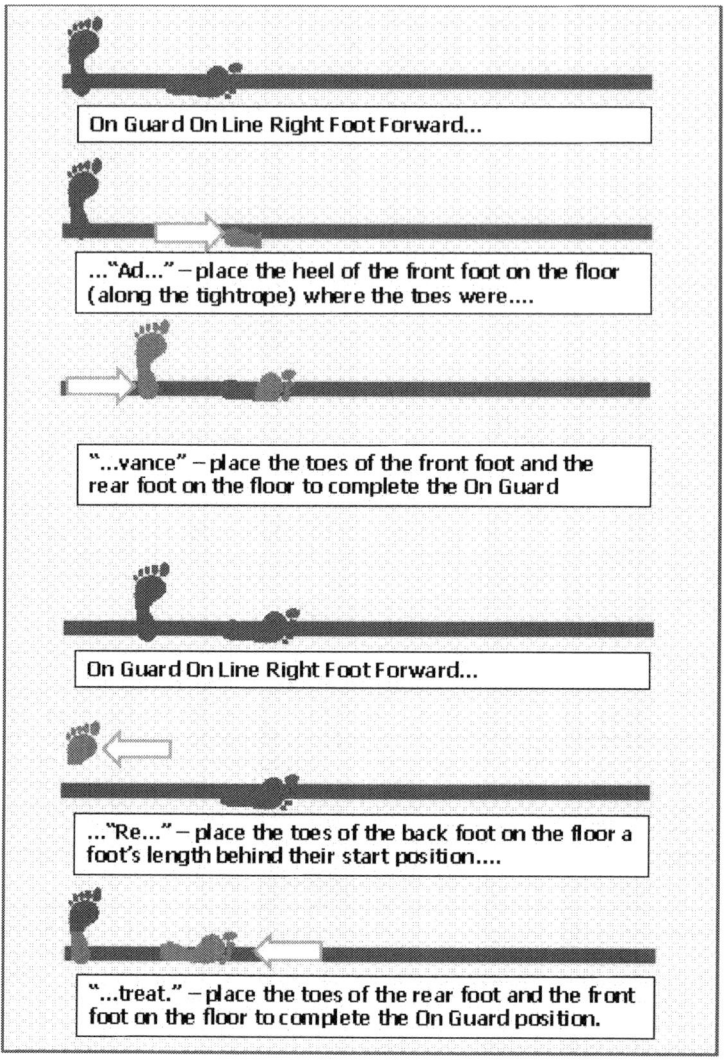

Diagram 4 – *Footprints showing the Advance and the Retreat*

Fingerwork 1 – Grip & Guards

What is it?

Anything you do with the sword hand. Or arm.

Confused? Let me try to explain.

Anything that is to do with the dexterous control of the weapon in question (let's say a sword) will be referred to as 'fingerwork'. This is in the hope that I imply that the work is from the fingers, which allows the sword to lead, and the arm/body/feet to follow.

The sword is an extension of your forefinger, not a separate entity, and it is to where you point that your sword will lead and your body will follow. In attack, your feet and body will follow after your blade and in defence your feet and body will yield according to your blade.

Fingerwork is important…

Let us begin with on guard.

'On guard' means that you are ready to attack or defend.

At this stage you have an on guard online position, with your sword nearer your partner than your body.

There is a choice of hand position: pronated, supinated, or something in between. Let us assume that you have a cutting edge to your sword. Let us imagine that the sword

Fingerwork 1 – Grip & Guards

is lying on a table in front of us; it has a sharp, cutting edge along one length and a blunt, back edge on the other. Our thumb being stronger than our fingers, is positioned opposite the cutting edge - pick up a sharp kitchen knife to slice onions and decide whether your thumb aligns with the sharp edge or the blunt back of the blade. Now, keeping the cutting edge to the outside of your body, and the thumb in opposition, you should find that the premier on guard position incorporates a pronated sword hand. So if anyone attacks you from the sword arm side they will encounter the sharp, cutting edge. An attack to your non-sword side, however, will involve twisting your sword hand through 180° in order to meet it with the cutting edge.

Why you should want to meet the oncoming attack edge to edge is dealt with more thoroughly in the section on parries.

On guard, as far as the fingers are concerned, fine tunes what the foot and body positions set up. The difference is that the fingers react directly to what your partner gives you in terms of sword position and attacks, and will change with them, while the rest of your on guard remains constant.

For example: Your partner may choose to come on guard and aim at a specific target – your sword arm bicep, for instance: you may choose to counteract their intent by engaging their blade with yours and holding it off-target –

so your blade would be inside theirs and your hand would be in a position outside of yours, so that if they extended their blade and moved it forward it would miss you to the outside. While your fingers have affected the defence, your body position will have remained unchanged.

Lines of Attack & Defence

Let us start by looking at Lines of Attack and Lines of Defence. In theory these are pretty infinite as you can be attacked from any direction and from any angle so let's simplify this a little by limiting these lines.

High Line – anything above the waist
Low Line – anything below the waist
Inside Line – body-side of the defenders sword arm
Outside Line – the unoccupied side of the defenders sword arm - where their body isn't

And to further refine-
High Line Targets – Middle of bicep and centre head
Low Line Targets – Hips

Targets may be attacked either by:
Straight line attacks with the point – **Thrusts**
Or by circular attacks with the cutting edge – **Cuts**.
These attacks must be blocked - or parried, or they may wound or kill.

Cuts, Thrusts & Parries are all led by the blade at the instigation of the fingers – any wrist/forearm/elbow/upper arm/shoulder/body

Fingerwork 1 – Grip & Guards

movement will be as a result of what the blade does/fingers do - NOT the driving force.

When referring to defence – or guards – we think in terms of 'zone defence' in that the high sword guard defends our pirate's top right quarter, the low non-sword guard defends his lower left quarter, etc. These should be fairly obvious, but there is often confusion with the terms…not surprising when you think that Stage Right=Opposite Prompt=Bastard Prompt=Camera Left…

Ensure that you, your partner, the class as a whole - and the teacher – are all using the same glossary: 'front somersault', for example, means entirely different things to English and American folks! "Two nations divided by a common language"…too true! Define the terms 'back flip', back roll', back somersault' and 'back handspring' in British English and American English, for instance. Even the last quote adds to the confusion as no-one appears to be sure whether it was George Bernard Shaw or Oscar Wilde who originally said it.

Sometimes these areas are referred to as high or low, inside or outside lines: for example 'high outside' = high sword side, and 'low inside' = low non-sword side. (Abbreviated to HI, HO, LI and LO). To avoid confusion, the inside line is the body side of the sword arm and the outside line is the non-body side. Another possible confusion here is that 'inside' in boxing and other fighting styles refers to distance.

Fingerwork 1 – Grip & Guards

Diagram 5 – Lines of Attack and Defence

- 1=lower non-sword quadrant;
- 2=lower sword side quadrant;
- 3= upper sword-side quadrant &
- 4= upper non-sword side quadrant.

Fingerwork 1 – Grip & Guards

Eight Guard Positions

When on guard with the feet, you will also assume an on guard position with the upper body, appropriate to the time, place & weapon. As mentioned above, the sword positions of on guard have the weapon covering a specific segment of the body – rather like a boxer whose left hand will cover the left side of his head and his right will protect the right.

The guard positions in sword fighting are based on the old French convention of enumeration and follow a loosely circular pattern: Prime, Seconde, Tierce, Quarte, Quinte, Sixte, Septime & Octave. Or One, Two, Three, Four, Five, Six, Seven & Eight

A reminder: 'guard', as in 'on guard' (or alternatively *'en garde'*), means 'ready to attack or defend'. None of the following are either offensive or defensive measures in themselves but preparatory positions from which to either launch an attack or execute a block, or parry.

The First Guard position of the sword corresponds to the quickest position arrived at upon unsheathing: place the hand on the grip of the scabbarded weapon and withdraw. As soon as the tip is clear, point it towards your opponent. This is a Guard of the Low Line on the Non-Sword Side and your easiest line of attack is to your partner's sword leg assuming they bear arms with the same hand – left or right – as you. Your sword-arm lies across your body as if you

Fingerwork 1 – Grip & Guards

were looking at a wristwatch. The hand position is pronated – you can see the main, punching, knuckles of the fist and not your fingernails.

The Second Guard position is achieved by drawing your sword hand across the front of your body to finish on the outside of the body line opposite the scabbard. This guard is still in the low line, now on the sword side of the body – the easiest attack from here would be to your opponent's non-sword leg. The hand is still pronated.

The Third Guard position is on the same – sword – side of the body but in the high line. Keeping the hand pronated, turn the sword just as if you were going from 'thumbs down' to 'thumbs up' in a Roman Arena, until the entire blade is outside your body on the sword side, above the hilt and point inclined towards your opponent. Assuming same-handedness, the direct line is to their non-sword arm.

The Fourth Guard position brings the sword hand across your body and off your non-sword side. In modern fencing, this guard is still pronated; however, a stronger (and more comfortable) position is achieved by allowing the hand to supinate, that is, allowing you to see the fingernails. Here you are covered in the high line, non-sword quadrant with a view to a simple, direct attack on your opponent's high line sword side.

Fingerwork 1 – Grip & Guards

The Fifth Guard position involves raising the sword hand above the head on the sword side with the point a little lower than the hilt and inclined toward the opposite sword shoulder – defence and attack position for the head. A dramatic, if limited, position, it's roots lie in the lighter, edged weapons, as opposed to the medieval broadswords of yore, and definitively used in German University Mensurschläger duelling.

The Sixth Guard is the supinated version of the third guard.

The Seventh Guard position is the supinated version of the first, and the **Eighth Guard** is the supinated form of the second.

These guard positions are interpreted in a variety of different ways dependent upon weapon, or weapons, being wielded.

Generally speaking, the classic 'on guard online' position has the sword in the third guard position.

The Sword

The time has come to finally pick up a sword. But what is it? Here, to help you not appear foolish and pick the thing up by the wrong end, is a brief guide to a basic sword.

The sword essentially comes in two parts:

Fingerwork 1 – Grip & Guards

- The **Blade** – the sharp bit you poke and slash with;
- The **Hilt** – the end you hold.

Both parts come in a vast variety of shapes and designs, mostly functional but some decorative. Here we will deal in general terms as an introduction to the weapon you may encounter when first you start. (This will be an 'ideal' starter sword; in reality you will find that compromises – mainly through cost – will be made, especially with the selection of blade.)

You will be learning to make cuts and to thrust: to that end the blade will be around 80cms in length and flat, like the cutlery knife you would eat with. Like the knife, one edge will be sharp. This is the 'cutting edge' or 'leading edge' or simply the 'edge'. The opposite edge will be blunt. The other two faces of the blade are referred to as the 'flat'. No part of the blade is ever referred to as the 'side'. The business end of the blade is the 'point' or 'tip'. The third of the sword from the tip down is the 'foible', or weakest part. This is the part of the sword that leads the attacks and is the part of the blade that is parried. The third of the blade from the hilt up is the 'forté', or strongest part. This is the part of the blade which makes the parries in defence. The middle section of the blade between the forté and the foible is called the 'middle section'.

Fingerwork 1 – Grip & Guards

The blade does not simply stop when it reaches the hilt but is cut in sharply at right angles – the 'shoulders' – and continues as a narrow finger called the 'tang', which passes through the length of the hilt and sticks out a little bit at the bottom. This protrusion is threaded and screwed onto what is called the 'nut' or 'pommel', which holds the thing together, as well as acting as a counterbalance for the blade. This should put the point of balance at a centimetre or two along the blade, up from the hilt.

Remember, this is the ideal sword; the reality is that you will be using a modern fencing blade. These are light, strong and flexible but it is not always apparent, when you first start, which is the cutting edge.

The hilt is essentially made up of two parts, the part which offers protection to the sword hand, and the part which the sword hand holds. The part which you hold is the 'handle' or 'grip'. The part which protects is called the 'guard'.

Entire chapters can and have been dedicated to the guard of the sword but at this stage we need only bother with two basic forms: one because it is the one you have seen and drawn as a child and the other because it is the one you will probably be using. A bar at right angles to the blade is the most rudimentary form of guard. This makes the sword look like a cross and therefore earns the sobriquet of 'cross guard'. Although this may be made

Fingerwork 1 – Grip & Guards

from one piece of metal, each projection is regarded as a separate entity, so technically, the cross guard is made up of two 'quillons'. The other type of guard is a 'cup guard'. This you may have seen on modern fencing weapons, the foil or the epée. These are both thrusting weapons and the cup is the most effective protection against this form of attack being like a very small, circular shield which is wedged between the handle and the shoulders. The handle is a tubular, hollow piece which slides onto the tang. It can be shaped or moulded but arguably the most useful to our purposes is the modern sport sabre grip. The sabre is a cutting as well as a thrusting weapon and the grip has a definite indentation for the thumb which gives a clear indication to the user which edge is the cutting edge of the blade. Incidentally it is not at all uncommon to have a cup guard *and* quillons on the hilt and indeed in some cases the leading quillon (corresponding with the leading edge) is stretched and curved back to the pommel to form a 'knuckle-guard'. The modern sabre guard has the cup and knuckle-guard format to protect from both cuts and thrusts, which is advantageous to the stage fighter both for the protection offered and the fact that, as the knuckle-guard aligns with the cutting edge of the blade, it helps to know how to hold the thing.

So the ideal weapon will be a light, single edged, pointed broadsword or rapier with a cup/quillon/knuckle-guard hilt: what you will have, however, will be an old foil, or if you are lucky, a modern sabre hilt attached to a maraging epée blade…

Fingerwork 1 – Grip & Guards

Here is a tour of a sword, starting from the pointy end:

- Tip or Point – sharp end used for thrusting into your opponent
- Leading or Cutting Edge – sharp edge, used for slicing into opponents
- Back of the Blade – blunt edge of the blade
- Back Edge – sharpened part of the Back of the Blade (maybe the top third)
- Double Edge – sword blade with both edges completely sharp
- Flat of the Blade – either of the two sides of the blade
- Foible – the third of the blade nearest the tip; the weakest part of the blade
- Forté – the third of the blade nearest the hilt; strongest part of the blade
- Middle Section – part of the blade between the forté and the foible
- Fuller – groove set into the Flat of the Blade; for strength and flexibility. Sometimes erroneously – but dramatically – referred to as the Blood Gutter
- Shoulders – where the blade narrows (usually at right angles) and the guard/hilt fits
- Tang – part of the blade which goes through the handle, the end of which is usually threaded to accommodate the…

Fingerwork 1 – Grip & Guards

- Pommel – basically the nut that holds the sword together; often used as a counterweight to the blade to provide for better balance and aid the heft of the sword; can be ornate and decorative
- Guard – structure designed to protect the sword hand/fingers: can range from the very plain and simple to the extremely intricate and ornate
- Quillons – on a cross-guard sword (the sword is cruciform) the quillons are the two short arms of the cross. Not always present. Can be large and recurved, as on a Scottish Claymore, with decorative ends; one quillon may be extended and curved back to connect with the pommel to form a
- Knuckle-guard – this may simply be a bar set at right-angles to the blade, or can be flattened out and rounded to protect the whole hand. This may be further embellished with piercings to become a Swept Hilt
- Cup Hilt – cup or glass-shaped guard (like a small bowl) which sits at right angles to the blade
- Ring Guard – one or two metal rings set above the quillon (sometimes also covered with a cup hilt) through which a finger may be hooked for better balance/control of the blade
- Handle or Grip – the part of the sword which is held

This list is by no means complete or exhaustive…

Fingerwork 1 – Grip & Guards

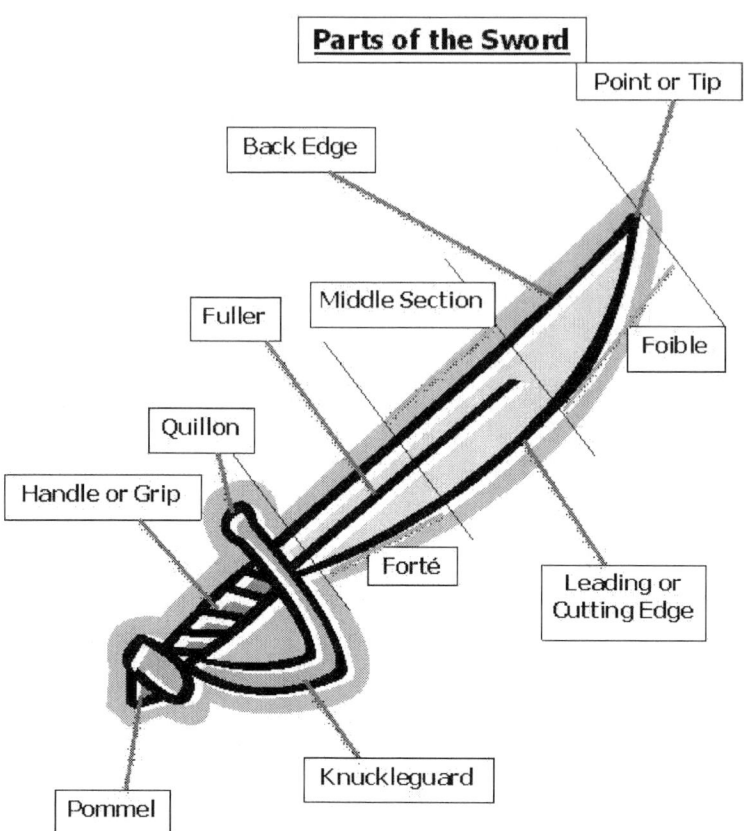

Diagram 6 – Parts of the Sword

How to Hold the Sword

Lay the sword on a table in front of you. The pommel should be nearest to you and the point aiming away from you. Shuffle to one side so that the handle aligns with your sword hand and your entire body is to one side of the sword. Ensure that the leading edge and knuckle-guard

Fingerwork 1 – Grip & Guards

(the sharp edge and the bow from cup to pommel) are on the outside. For a right handed person the body will be to the left of the sword and the sharp edge will be facing right.

Pronate the hand and let the open palm hover over the handle. Wrap your fingers around the handle so that the middle knuckles of the fingers align with the knuckle-guard. Place the pad of your thumb on the handle on the opposite side to the knuckle-guard. Gently pick up the sword.

How tight to hold it? "Hold your sword as if you were holding a bird in your hand: not too lightly to prevent his escape and not too tightly to prevent him choking." *(Fencing enthusiast Justin Lafauger, 1826)*
You don't want to drop it but it's no white-knuckle ride.

NOTE: Be flexible. The preceding is intended as a guide. How you will find to hold your weapon will be a matter of personal choice influenced by factors such as the weight, heft, grip, attack, defence etc. Personally I constantly adjust my grip while I am fighting: the important thing is to be in control and to be relaxed.

So you have your sword in your hand; assume the (on guard) position and prepare for the next lesson:

The Extension

A threat, a preparation and an attack in itself, the extension is a vital, fundamental sword-fighting technique. It is as

Fingerwork 1 – Grip & Guards

simple as it can be, so beware the temptation to embellish or enhance it – it requires no additives.

From the on guard position, simply straighten the sword-arm level with the shoulder. That's it. The feeling should be as if someone standing directly in front of you has taken hold of your straightened index finger and very gently and smoothly pulled it to draw your arm straight. Refined to perfection, allow the hand to pronate completely so that the palm is facing the ground, permit the wrist to be slightly higher than the shoulder and the straight index finger to drop slightly to maintain its lock on the target of your partner's navel.

The extension is the thrust attack: an attack made with the point of the sword.

Finding Targets

Now with sword in hand assume the third guard: imagine that you are opposite your evil twin and that they are facing you at your mercy, unarmed, square on and with their arms hanging down at their sides. Check that your on guard position – which now includes a sword – ticks all the boxes. Also ensure that your sword point is in line with partner's navel - not aimed or directed at, but *level* with. The audience visualises movement as left to right or right to left: they are not very good at following lines of blades. Help them as much as possible.

Fingerwork 1 – Grip & Guards

Now switch your gaze and focus on their arm, the arm which is on your sword side. If you are right handed it would be their left. Focus specifically on the bicep at a point midway between elbow and shoulder. Extend and as you do, allow your point to drift up and come on line with that spot on their arm. Being your twin they would hold the sword in the same hand as you, so this would be their non-sword side. You would be aiming at their fourth guard position. Recover the sword back to on guard. Now look out another target; the other arm, perhaps. Extend to the mid-point on that bicep – what would be their sword arm. You are extending into their third guard position. The hip at the point where the thigh joins the pelvis on the same side, their sword side, will have you extending to their second guard position, and finally a violation of their first guard would see you extending to the non-sword hip. Practice these extensions slowly. Feel the difference between a neutral On Guard state and a focussed, threatening extended state. Try to feel that the tip of your sword is connected to each specific target by a length of elastic which draws the point towards the target, the sword *then* the arm following into extension. And ensure that it is only the sword and arm…that there is no movement at the shoulder, no leaning forward from the waist into the extension, no hint of trying to force the extension by 'punching' it out from the shoulder. The extension is drawn *from* you, not pushed *by* you. Each target is very specifically located – if there were a laser beam from the

Fingerwork 1 – Grip & Guards

point of the sword it would unwaveringly hit the same square centimetre of target in each guard every time.

Footwork 2 - Lunge & Recover

Lunge & Recover

This section deals with the lunge and takes a closer look at the recover.

You will by now have mastered the basics covered in Footwork 1 and refined your sword arm technique in Fingerwork. Now we start to bring it all together...

The Lunge

The Lunge can be used offensively as part of a thrusting or cutting attack with the sword, or it can be used defensively as an avoidance – remember these two distinctions and you will see why the lunge comes under the 'Footwork' section of Sword Fighting.

The lunge is basically a large step – how large will be defined by it meeting several strict mechanical requirements, and in which direction will depend on its application and the choreographic requirements.

Let us assume that we are using the Lunge in its attack mode. We are nicely on guard online and have selected the thrust attack. We have extended. Now we are ready to Lunge. *NB in attack mode the lunge is ALWAYS led by the blade: never lunge first and then try to cut or thrust for, by that time, you will have merely succeeded in bravely throwing yourself onto your opponent's point...*

Footwork 2 - Lunge & Recover

So, you have extended, it is safe to continue with your attack, and you lunge:

1. take a large step forwards with the front foot, along the on guard line, by pushing off your rear leg;
2. the heel of the front foot lands first immediately followed by the toes.

The finished position has the front foot flat, foot and shin at right angles to each other, with the leading knee directly over the heel. Having either the foot ahead of the knee or the knee over the toes, or further, are to be avoided as in both cases you will require an extra weight shift before you can move that front foot back again to recover. The rear leg is straight and the back foot is flat on the floor and definitely not rolled onto the inside. The body is absolutely upright, not even a hint of lean, forwards, backwards or to either side.

At the same time as you push off the rear foot into the lunge, allow the non-sword arm to lower to a position parallel with the rear leg, palm uppermost. This helps balance and is now in a position to help with the recover.

Footwork 2 - Lunge & Recover

Diagram 7 – The Lunge

Recover back to on guard by pushing off the front foot and simultaneously raising the non-sword arm back to its original position. Fractionally behind everything else, bring the sword arm back from the extended position to the on guard.

Throughout the entire process of extend, lunge & recover the head will have moved only in a straight line, forwards and backwards, with the body – no independent nods or inclinations. Most importantly, it will not have bobbed up and down, as the most efficient lunges slide into and out of position horizontally, with motion only in that one plane – not vertically.

Footwork 2 - Lunge & Recover

Let us take time out to examine and define the term 'recover'.

The definition is very strict and thus very simple: *To return to on guard.* So when you lunge by stepping forward with the front foot you recover by bringing that foot back to its original position.

If you are in the unfortunate position of being lunged at by an extended sword, you have two basic choices on the 'fight or flight' principle – run away (avoidance) or deflect it (parry). Avoidances we will look at later, but right now…

Fingerwork 2 - Parries

Parries

The parry is a defensive move to counter an attack made by the opponent's blade by blocking or deflecting its course to the target.

Parries protect the same four body quadrants, and the head, as the guard positions do. They also follow the same numbering convention.

Parry 1 – Sword vertical, point down, Non-Sword Side, Low Line, hand pronated.

Parry 2 – Sword vertical, point down, Sword Side, Low Line, hand pronated.

Parry 3 – Sword vertical, point up, Sword Side, High Line, hand pronated.

Parry 4 – Sword vertical, point up, Non-Sword Side, High Line, hand supinated.

Parry 5 – Sword horizontal overhead, point to Non-Sword Side, hand pronated.

Parry 5a – Sword horizontal overhead, point to Sword Side, hand supinated.

Parry 6 - Sword vertical, point up, Sword Side, High Line, hand supinated.

Fingerwork 2 - Parries

Parry 7 - Sword vertical, point down, Non-Sword Side, Low Line, hand supinated.

Parry 8 – Sword vertical, point down, Sword Side, Low Line, hand supinated.

This dry summation of the sword/hand positions is, however, but a small part of the story: the important part is the transitions...

The Path of the Parry

This is the part to spend time over. And over. And over again. But first we must disarm and look with loin ungirded back into the realm of unarmed.

> *"Wax On, Wax Off..."* (Mr. Miyagi's to Daniel-san *The Karate Kid, 1984, Columbia Pictures*)

How do blocks work? What makes a block successful? More to the point, how do we guarantee the success of a block?

The block has the same definition as a parry - to deflect or stop an attack reaching its target. In terms that are most accessible, and therefore easiest to visualise, let us hypothesise with a punch to the body. Assuming that we are frozen to the spot and able only to move our arms, how do we stop a punch from reaching us? It depends on the punch: Do we need to block it or deflect it? That would depend on whether it was coming at us in a straight line from the front or curving in to us from the side.

Fingerwork 2 - Parries

Coming in on a straight line – let us assume from the right shoulder of a right-handed puncher to the left shoulder of the victim – the attack has to be deflected, but with which arm? Let us alter slightly our way of thinking about this conundrum and view it rather as 'danger' and 'safe'. If we imagine that our body is red – the danger zone where contact will equate to pain, and the space around us is green – if the attacker hits that - thereby missing me - I won't get hurt… Then all we have to do is work out how to move an attack aimed at the red zone into the green zone. And to refine this a little more, by the shortest, safest route.

Back to this punch: it is coming in on a straight line to our left shoulder – our very red left shoulder. Where is the nearest green space? Answer: just to the left side of our left shoulder, or just above it. Question: is there a safer option of the two? Answer: above the shoulder is nearer to our face and thus more dangerous, so it must be to the side. So what is the most efficient way of deflecting the punch from red to green?

Imagine someone standing in front of you. They lightly grip your left upper arm in their right hand, how would you push that hand off? Answer: either by crossing your body with your right hand and pushing the arm away from you, or by circling your left arm inward and upwards so that it too crosses in front your body before connecting with the unwanted arm and pushing it away. What you are

Fingerwork 2 - Parries

not doing – in either case – is coming in from the outside of the unwanted arm and trying to push it through your own body into the green zone to your right.

Understand this fundamental concept about blocking and the following section will fall easily into place.

Unarmed 1 - Blocked Punch Exercise

Punching & Blocking Exercise

The following is an exercise to drill pair work, timing, coordination, targeting, rhythm, eye-contact and safety technique. It is NOT a lesson in throwing 'real'-looking stage punches. When you try this, use it for what it is, an exercise to practice certain specific elements. Do not try to make this look like a fight or realistic punching.

That comes later.

First practice each side of the exercise by yourself:

A: stand with feet hip-width apart, neither foot forward of the other. Bend the arms so the elbows are flexed at about 90° and the forearms are parallel to the ground.

Make loose fists – the thumbs should be on top and the fingernails of each hand will be on the inside, facing each other. If you were to open your hands at this point you would look ready to clap.

Now extend one fist forwards in a slow punch. I will guarantee that as your arm extends it rotates a quarter of a revolution and that by the time it is fully extended the fist is pronated so that the back of the hand is uppermost and the knuckles are in a row instead of a column. This is a very natural action but one that must be resisted for the purposes of this exercise.

Unarmed 1 - Blocked Punch Exercise

The drill is simply to extend alternate arms with hands in loose, relaxed fists, bringing the first arm back as you extend the second. It doesn't look, or feel, like fighting and it shouldn't…more like an awkward dance!

Stand opposite B and look at where their biceps and hips are; these will be your four targets. Remember that the biceps are assumed to be in their usual place when the arms are relaxed, on either side of B's body, and that B isn't waving their arms wildly in the air.

The first punch will be with the right and will travel towards B's left bicep. Slowly extend the right arm and check that you are too far apart to actually touch the target; ideally your fist should stop about 20cm short of the bicep when the arm is fully extended.

At this stage B does nothing other than stand and provide targets for A who should find a gentle rhythm (count and-one-and-two-and-three-and-four etc.) no faster than an old grandfather clock (and-tick-and-tock-and-tick-and-tock…). The first slow punch should arrive at B's left bicep on 'one'. The right arm immediately starts to withdraw as the left gently extends to B's right bicep, arriving on 'two'. *(Targets: the convention is to name targets from the defender's point of view so "punch left shoulder" refers to the defender's left shoulder NOT the shoulder on the left as viewed by the attacker, which [normally] would be the defender's right shoulder).*

Unarmed 1 - Blocked Punch Exercise

'Three' is the right extending in the low line for B's left hip and 'four' sees the left fist aiming towards the right hip. Repeat this pattern three times. Practice this until you have a relaxed, gentle and rhythmical dance going on.

Now to B, the 'other' side:

B: Stand in the same start position but with the hands open and relaxed, palms down; now bring the left hand across the waist so that the fingers almost touch the inside of the right elbow.

From the right side of the body, bring the forearm up to vertical, keeping the left elbow where it is, on the left waist. There is a great possibility that you have turned your hand on the way up as if to wave to someone in front of you. Resist that urge! The palm is facing the floor; as the arm raises, lead with the back of the hand so that when it is vertical, from your point of view, all you can see is the palm of the hand to the left of your head. You should not be able to see the back of the hand at all. Having got to this position it is most important that you LEAVE THE HAND WHERE IT IS.

Now repeat with the right – bring the hand across your body, continue to raise the forearm so the hand wipes across in front of your face, finishing with the hand to the right of the head, palm facing you, and LEAVE IT THERE. You now have your hands up in the classic fishing 'one that got away' pose!

Unarmed 1 - Blocked Punch Exercise

The next stage is to lower the left hand: take it back the way it came, so wipe it across and down past your face until the thumb can touch the right side of the waist. Continue the movement in this circular direction until the hand just passes the leg. You should be looking at the back of the hand, the thumb able to point towards your left thigh. Describe a similar semi-circle with the right arm to complete the sequence.

To repeat, simply reverse the semi-circles. You will feel (and look) like the original 1978 Space Invaders once you get this little dance going..!

The trick with this part is to not move the arm until it is needed…

This is a deceptively simple exercise which is easy to abuse and all I can say is that it is worth spending as long as it takes to ensure that everything is in place and all the lessons this little gem has to offer have been learned…

Now to put both parts together: First, some explanation; take your arms in the start position and make loose fists. Now cross your forearms a la 'The X Factor'. Now GENTLY knock the touching edges of your arms together. Even with only the lightest of bumps there is a disproportionately high amount of pain…

This is why the punches mustn't rotate and the blocks mustn't be waves. The soft, fleshy inner side of the

Unarmed 1 - Blocked Punch Exercise

punching forearm should be met by the flat and forgiving outer side of the blocking arm.

At the correct distance apart where the punches are 20cm short there is obviously no need to block because they can't actually connect – if there was no block, nothing would happen.

Because B doesn't need to block, there doesn't need to be any rush – instead, time must be taken for the two of you to find a common rhythm; the first block arrives at the same time (technically, a fraction after) as the first punch does. The punch is aimed at the left bicep – the target is 'hot', glowing red. The block should meet the punch and following the making of a very gentle contact, the blocker should continue moving the arm a little further until the fist is pointing at the 'green' (safe) space to the side of the target. The movement of the fist from on-target to off-target marks the success of the block and the failure of the attack; the punch then starts to withdraw and the second punch gently extends to the right bicep. The left blocking arm stays where it is while the right block gently swings up to meet and move the second punch; the second punch begins its withdrawal (defender is standing in the angler pose) and the third punch – right hand to left hip – starts forward. By leaving the arm in the first block position, we have removed any options of travel to the left, low line block position; it can only travel in an inside semi-circle, meet the attack and move it gently out of harm's way to

Unarmed 1 - Blocked Punch Exercise

the side of the thigh. (Taking the outside semicircle would mean the left hand travelling out and away from the head instead of passing downwards and in front of it. The block would then meet the punch; however, instead of guiding the attack away to the side of the target it would bring the attack further onto the target – a failed block...)

Finally the low right punch withdraws as the low left moves in and the blocking right arm begins its journey from vertical fingers up, inside and down 180° to vertical fingers down, meeting & moving the attack off the red and into the green.

Eye-contact – it is possible to maintain eye-contact throughout, however, I would recommend that you start to get into the habit of:

1. Eye-contact at the start – checking & cueing
2. Attacker then moves eyes to the target to
    a. ensure their own accuracy and
    b. to reinforce to the defender exactly where they are going.
3. Resume eye-contact as soon as the attack has failed to check *then* 'cue & go' with the next step.

And so on until the end of the sequence. Remember: eye-contact before and after each move, target and safety checks during the move.

Fingerwork 3 – Path of the Parry

The Path of the Parry (cont'd...)

To get into the swing, as it were, let us assume the guard of three. Your opponent extends towards your non-sword bicep. At extending distance, their point comes to a stop some 20cms from your arm but on line. (If they were to take a step forward it would prod you in the centre point of the bicep). Now allow the point of your sword to drift a little further out to your sword side; further, further – your forearm may drift a little too, but the elbow does not move. Although it is your fingers that are doing the work, let it feel as if you are being led by the point. Now, just at the point when your sword hand has to turn out to prevent your upper arm from following, start to raise the point in a long, graceful arc until the blade is vertical; your Sword Hand will be supinated at this time (check that you can see the fingernails...) and now bring the hilt of the sword across your stomach, keeping the blade vertical above it. This action, like pulling a curtain closed in front of you, or wiping your windscreen with a very long windscreen wiper, should connect the forté of your blade to the foible of your partner's. Carry on in this line by allowing your shoulders to turn with you and your sword will gently guide your partner's point off the red zone of your bicep and into the adjacent green zone, where if your partner were now to take a step forward, the blade would pass harmlessly to your non-sword side.

Fingerwork 3 – Path of the Parry

Once your partner has recovered their sword back to on guard, you too may recover, retracing the exact same path forged on your outward journey.

Let me labour this point a little further: imagine that you are on guard in three in front of a large pane of glass that faces you like a wall, touching your point; as you drift your point out and backwards until it is nearly at right angles to your sword side and parallel to the floor, this glass wall is now only the length of your forearm in front of you. Without breaking the glass, you arc and traverse your sword into the position of your parry. After your partner has recovered, keep the sword vertical so that you do not break the glass on the return until your sword is out to your sword side, when the wall recedes before your point as your sword returns to third guard.

Why take this long, convoluted, laborious route? Is there not a quicker way to get to this parry? Why, yes there is! Simply whip your point up on a diagonal line and take the blade to vertical as you go. Your partner, by now, will have left the room. And if they try the same move on you, you will realise why: the shortest journey from third guard to this parry position involves taking the point of your sword straight across your partner's face…

And herein lays the one twenty-four carat Golden, Unbreakable, and Intractable Rule of Stage Sword Fighting:

Fingerwork 3 – Path of the Parry

THE POINT NEVER, EVER CROSSES THE LINE OF THE FACE.

So, as you practise, learn slowly, thoroughly and precisely from the start, the various Paths of the Parries. Wherever your sword is to begin with (and learn all parries at first from third guard) there will always be:

1. **The Preparation.**
2. **The Path.**
3. **The Parry.**
4. **The Recovery** – *but not until it is safe!*

Numbering the Parries

To be fair, we could call the parries anything we liked, however, the convention to which this author subscribes is that of a system of numbers corresponding to the guard positions.

As we have seen, the Guards are numbered in a circular fashion – following the easiest route – from a logical first position. To keep life simple, the parries are numbered according to the guards they protect; for example, fourth guard, on the non-sword high line is matched with the block called parry 4, a defence against an attack to the non-sword high line. Remember that the numbers are always from the defender's point of view.

Now let us look at the rest of the pathways.

Fingerwork 3 – Path of the Parry

In each case we will be on guard in, and recover back to, the third guard – 'on guard in three'. In each case, the preparation takes the point of the sword to the opposite side relative to the final parry position. And in each case, the final parry position will be the best compromise between pushing the sword out to the side and pushing it out directly in front of you – to the side to deflect the incoming blade as far as possible from the red to the green, and in front to ensure that the incoming blade is actually met – *note that you will be at a distance far enough apart from your partner as to prevent actual contact and this will need to be taken into account by closing the distance between the blades with the parry.*

1. **The Path to Parry 1**
    - 1.i. Drift the point out to the Sword Side.
    - 1.ii. Drop the point towards the floor, the blade vertical.
    - 1.iii. Draw the pronated hand across the body to the Non-Sword Side, meet and make safe the blade.
    - 1.iv. Following the Recovery of the attacker, recover back the way you came.
2. **The Path to Parry 2**
    - 2.i. Drift the point out to the Non-Sword Side.
    - 2.ii. Drop the point towards the floor, the blade vertical.
    - 2.iii. Draw the pronated hand across the body to the Sword Side, meet and make safe the blade.

Fingerwork 3 – Path of the Parry

2.iv. Following the Recovery of the attacker, recover back the way you came.

3. **The Path to Parry 3**
    3.i. Drift the point out to the Non-Sword Side.
    3.ii. Raise the point towards the sky, the blade vertical.
    3.iii. Draw the pronated hand across the body to the Sword Side, meet and make safe the blade.
    3.iv. Following the Recovery of the attacker, recover back the way you came.

4. **The Path to Parry 4**
    4.i. Drift the point out to the Sword Side.
    4.ii. Raise the point towards the sky, the blade vertical.
    4.iii. Draw the supinated hand across the body to the Non-Sword Side, meet and make safe the blade.
    4.iv. Following the Recovery of the attacker, recover back the way you came.

The following is more for information and reference purposes as these parries are not relevant at this stage and you should be concentrating on the first four.

5. **The Path to Parry 6**
    5.i. Drift the point out to the Non-Sword Side.
    5.ii. Raise the point towards the sky, the blade vertical.
    5.iii. Draw the supinated hand across the body to the Sword Side, meet and make safe the blade.

Fingerwork 3 – Path of the Parry

    5.iv. Following the Recovery of the attacker, recover back the way you came.

6. **The Path to Parry 7**
   - 6.i. Drift the point out to the Sword Side.
   - 6.ii. Drop the point towards the floor, the blade vertical.
   - 6.iii. Draw the supinated hand across the body to the Non-Sword Sid, meet and make safe the blade.
   - 6.iv. Following the Recovery of the attacker, recover back the way you came.

7. **The Path to Parry 8**
   - 7.i. Drift the point out to the Non-Sword Side.
   - 7.ii. Draw the supinated hand across the body to the Sword Side, meet and make safe the blade.
   - 7.iii. Following the recovery of the attacker, recover back the way you came.

Important Notes on the Parries:

It is worth repeating that in each and every case the route begins with the sword point drifting out to the opposite side to where the parry is destined. This movement clears the point of your sword away from your incoming partner's lunge, and also gives them a clear signal that you have seen their attack preparation and are ready with the corresponding parry. The parry is to make you safe, but it begins by ensuring the safety of your partner. It also reinforces 'cue & go' and 'victim control'.

Fingerwork 3 – Path of the Parry

These are 'lateral' parries having limited sword arm movement left and right, no up and down movement at all. The raising and lowering of the sword point is produced by the fingers, helped by a loose wrist.

It is also worth repeating the note regarding final blade positions and distance, which is a tricky concept to grasp at this stage without an opponent in front of you – remember that you will be fighting 'out of distance' (see the next chapter), that is, too far apart to actually make the hit. This means that if you are finishing your parry straight out to the side of your body you will slip off the incoming blade or not reach it at all, rendering it dangerous as you thereby allow it the freedom to enter your red zone. If your final blade position is straight out in front of you, you will still be exposing part of your body to the incoming blade – in other words, your parry will not have cleared your own body and moved out into the green zone. You need to find a position that is halfway between being out to the side and directly in front of you. Now, this is relatively easy with the sword side parries (2, 3 & 8) as you merely have to allow your hand to drift away from your body to find the safe position. However for those parries to the non-sword side (1, 4 & 7) you will have to allow your shoulders to turn almost forty-five degrees which will both push your parrying blade further across your body into safety while at the same time pulling your target area backwards and away from attack.

Imagine that you are standing in an alleyway with walls running its length on either side of you about 50cms away from your torso on each side, and then you must touch these walls with your middle knuckles on each parry.

Fingerwork 3 – Path of the Parry

Low Line Parry Practice

A simple, useful exercise (which can be developed and built on as you progress) is this:

1. Come on guard in three;
2. Drift sword to sword side, turn hand to drop the point, and gently move the blade across to parry 1, pushing the sword with your thumb (which should be aligned with the back edge of the blade).
3. Hold for a moment and check the integrity of the parry – has it cleared your body and is it pushed as far out in front of you as it can be without leaning the body forward (remember balance).
4. Move the blade back to the sword side – keeping point down – and with a gentle twist of the wrist bring the blade back to third guard.

This is the beginnings of building your default parrying programme into your physical memory – do it slowly, smoothly and consistently.

When you are happy with your progress on 1, move on to 2. Don't be too happy too quickly – these (permit the drama!) are the moves that will save your life!

1. From third guard, drift the point out to the non-sword side, drop the point and, with your thumb in line with the back edge of the blade, use the thumb to push the sword out and in front of your body until you arrive smoothly and positively to the position of parry 2.

Fingerwork 3 – Path of the Parry

2. In keeping with the rules of the game, retrace the path back to recovery in third.

Yes it is quicker and more economical and just as safe to recover by drifting the point out to the sword side and back into guard but this begins the development of a very bad habit: the danger with continuing the move, instead of stopping at the parry position and retracing the path, is that you form the blueprint of one continuous, circular move which, if mistimed, may pass the parry position before the attacking blade has arrived, and resume the guard position as your partner completes their lunge, both impaling themselves on your point whilst simultaneously running your sword leg through with theirs! Not good things.

NOTE: Each and every time you move the sword in a circular motion as you perform a defensive manoeuvre – parry – circle it as if you are standing in front of the glass wall. Or, if there was an axle connecting your navel to that of your partner, and a huge cart wheel fixed to it, then your point would follow the line of its rim, never getting closer to your partner until the very end when you resume your guard. (Circling the sword with the point moving towards your partner is an attacking move and will be covered later in this manual).

This next stage is pedantic and time consuming when all you will want to do is race ahead to learn the next parry. Discipline yourself. This is the start of a system of working which will pay big dividends in the future. Trust me!

Fingerwork 3 – Path of the Parry

On Guard in Third Guard
1. Go to Parry 1.
2. Pause.
3. Recover to Third Guard.
4. Pause.
5. Go to Parry 2.
6. Pause.
7. Recover to Third Guard.
8. Pause.

Repeat slowly smoothly and consistently ten times or until you can perform the movement EXACTLY the same each time. You will begin to find that the level of concentration required to achieve and maintain consistency is surprisingly intense.

Until such time arrives when these moves have become second nature – embedded in your physical memory – you are not ready to progress; for, when you encounter this exercise in practice, you cannot afford the time to learn it again, you must know it.

Fingerwork 3 – Path of the Parry

High Line Parry Practice

This is the same exercise applied to Parries 3 & 4.

Drift the point to the non-sword side and raise the point to vertical. With the blade vertical, bring the hand back across the body to the sword side and into the parry position of 3. Pause and check. Then bring the upright blade back across the body with a move of the hand. When the sword gets to the non-sword side, drop the point outwards in a big arc, take it all back to the sword side and recover to guard three.

Now onto 4: drift the point to the sword side. Arc it out and up to vertical. Now move the hand and upright blade across the body – allowing the shoulders to twist – into parry 4. Pause and check. Move the upright sword back to sword side and arc it back to guard 3.

And now the exercise:

On Guard in the Third Guard.
1. Go to Parry3.
2. Pause.
3. Recover to Third Guard.
4. Pause.
5. Go to Parry 4.
6. Pause.
7. Recover to Third Guard.
8. Pause.
9. Repeat until perfect.

Fingerwork 3 – Path of the Parry

The next step is to put the two exercises together. This depends crucially on two things. That you have previously rehearsed the first part to the extent that you do not have to think about it when you now go back to it; and that you are confident and comfortable enough with the new part that you don't throw yourself by doing the old bit first. This system of learning takes time at the beginning stages, but will allow you to progress with a greater degree of confidence and success as you go. Before you start, here is today's Top Tip: focus on the sword arm as if it were trapped in a letterbox slit – it must remain parallel to the ground, hinged from the elbow in such a way that it can only move laterally. Any circles are made with the fingers and wrist.

Start position – OG in 3

1. Go to Parry 1.
2. Pause.
3. Recover to Third Guard.
4. Pause.
5. Go to Parry 2.
6. Pause.
7. Recover to Third Guard.
8. Pause
9. Go to Parry 3.
10. Pause.
11. Recover to Third Guard.
12. Pause.

Fingerwork 3 – Path of the Parry

13. Go to Parry 4.
14. Pause.
15. Recover to Third Guard.
16. Pause.
17. Repeat all.

The first few/many times you attempt all of this you will become brain-fried, frustrated and surprised at how many mistakes you make. The trick here is not to try to cover up or correct the mistakes quickly, rather to stop, go back to the previous guard and slowly try the move again. Also, monitor your breathing. You will find yourself holding your breath and simply forgetting to breathe, such is the concentration required for the precise and accurate success of the exercise. The holding of breath is a clear and sure indicator of tension – the act of holding one's breath during exercise will create and/or add to the tension. By thinking about the breathing and working at keeping it relaxed and regular you not only help the breathing and the assist the releasing/avoiding of tension, but can also help relax the mind and stop it from concentrating too much and becoming preoccupied with the moves…

Practice this exercise until you can do it whilst singing a favourite song or reciting some lines – this helps the breathing/relaxation/tension syndromes – and remember that eventually you will be doing all this stuff as another character, in costume & make-up, under lights, with an

Fingerwork 3 – Path of the Parry

audience, and acting high emotions. But that is a long way away at this stage!

So you can:

Come On Guard
Advance
Retreat
Extend to four targets
Lunge
Recover
Parry in four positions.

You are now ready to face your first opponent… but before you do, you must learn about distance.

Distance – Defining & Checking

DISTANCE – DEFINING & CHECKING

The word "distance" has a very specific definition in stage combat (as it does in all fighting forms). It refers to the space between two fighting parties.

There are two basic flavours of distance – 'In Distance' and 'Out of Distance' and are defined as follows:

- In Distance – where the space between you and your opponent allows actual contact with the weapon you are using.
- Out of Distance – where the space between you and your opponent is too wide to enable contact, any attack would fall short of its target.

'Distance' is a vital concept, on several levels, not least in terms of safety, and must be drilled until it becomes second nature. Some will understand it and be able to apply it quicker than others in the same way that some people have natural hand/eye coordination or natural soccer skills but everyone can – and must – learn it.

Stand in front of your partner. Raise the palm of your right hand to their left cheek. If you can touch the cheek without moving your feet then you are in distance to slap them. If you cannot reach them, then you are out of distance. It is that simple. However, 'simple' does not mean 'easy'. What we have just defined is 'Slapping

Distance – Defining & Checking

Distance' as the open palm is the weapon and the cheek is the target. Clench your fist and you subtly change the distance as it foreshortens by several centimetres – in other words, for the fist to connect with the same target you need to stand a few centimetres closer. Or you change the distance by leaning in towards your partner a little. This facility to close distance by posture, i.e. without having to alter the foot position, must be noted and taken into account. It is a natural tendency and can be dangerous both as a subliminal method of making contact and as a device which can sufficiently alter your balance as to destabilise you. (*Closing* and *Opening* Distance – defined as 'moving nearer to' and 'moving farther from' your partner. In real fighting terms you would close the distance in order to connect with a blow and open the distance so as not to get hit. Although it is worth mentioning that closing the distance can also be a useful defensive technique: you can be just as safe – and potentially more dangerous – if you move *inside* your opponents distance… think of a right hook landing in the air behind your head as your forehead finds your opponent's nose, for example).

So this is 'slapping distance' and 'punching distance'; what if you were to kick your partner?

Your legs are considerably longer than your arms. So here we have 'kicking distance'. Each and every weapon – palm, fist, toe, knee, elbow, forehead, teeth – has its own distance requirements in order for it to make contact, and

Distance – Defining & Checking

sound if you find yourself NOT at the correct distance. But first things first:

To check Extending Distance: Stand opposite your partner, both of you on guard. One of you will lower their point, drifting it out to the side. The other will draw their sword back parallel to the floor until it is at right angles to you and your partner. (Stood on the compass, you and partner occupy North and South whilst the sword lies East-West between you.) The Checker will now slowly start to uncoil their arm to extension without leaning forward. The point of the sword is the last thing to come on line. If it is able to come on line without touching the other person, and it is the requisite 30-40cms short of their body, then the distance is about right. If either party feels that the distance requires adjustment, the sword is withdrawn, then the feet of ONE of you will make the adjustment (preferably the checkee) and the checker checks again. When both of you are happy with the distance, metaphorically glue your back feet to the floor. Neither foot *should* move, but, please note, it is the position of the *rearmost* foot which sets the distance (assuming that your on guard is consistent.)

To check Lunging Distance: Stand opposite your partner, both of you on guard. One of you will lower their point, drifting it out to the side. The other will draw their sword back parallel to the floor until it is at right angles to you and your partner. (Stood on the compass, you and

Distance – Defining & Checking

partner occupy North and South whilst the sword lies East-West between you.) The Checker will now lunge (remember, the lunge is a piece of footwork). It is essential that this test lunge is the longest, fullest and bestest lunge the checker can make – do not just mark the test with a lazy demi-lunge and then surprise your partner in the exercise. Bear in mind that it may be them lunging at you first. In the lunge, slowly start to uncoil the arm to extension without leaning forward. The point of the sword is the last thing to come online. If it is able to come online without touching the other person, and it is the requisite 30-40cms short of their body, then the distance is about right. If *either* party feels that the distance requires adjustment, then the checker remains in the lunge and the feet of the checkee will make the adjustment. Once both of you are happy with the distance, metaphorically glue your back feet to the floor. The classic mistake with this is that check is done meticulously, the parties recover and then one or other person steps forward to ask "Is that all right for you..?"

Extending and Parrying (Again!)

You've done this. You have extended to the four guards and you have parried 1, 2, 3 & 4. (Also 6, 7, & 8). Now all you need is a partner with the same level of expertise as you, who has also studied the section on Distance, and away you go.

Stand opposite each other.

Distance – Defining & Checking

One of you checks for extending distance. (Traditionally this will be the person who is first going to extend (again traditionally referred to as 'A') while the other will be doing the parries (To continue with tradition, they are 'B').

As part of the checking process, it is worth the checkee making the appropriate parry to ensure that it is attacking foible to parrying forté which connect without either party having to readjust, in particular, the person making the parry should not have to raise or lower their sword forearm, nor should they get into the habit of meeting and beating the opposing blade. Do not go 'out to bat' to connect with the attack, merely request greater accuracy and that the attacker wait for the defender's blade to move the offensive point from red to green.

Gentle consistency is all we seek: the attacker's job is to extend to the target and stay there until the defender's blade meets it and politely moves it to safety. If the attacking blade is coming in too high, do not quietly follow it and start raising your parries as, once you are in the habit of parrying high, the attacker will have a sudden fit of memory and thrust on target, which is now undefended.

When you are both happy with the distance, both come on guard in third guard.

1. Eye-contact
2. A – Move eyes to B's sword side hip
3. A – Extend to B's guard one
4. Pause & eye-contact
5. B – Moves to parry 1 position
6. Pause & eye-contact

Distance – Defining & Checking

7. A – Recovers to on guard (third)
8. Pause & eye-contact
9. B – Recovers to on guard (third)
10. Eye-contact
11. Pause

This exercise is written out laboriously and should be likewise performed. The reasons are thus:

Eye-contact – the first, last and everything-in-between safety of stage combat. A look conveys a thousand words. A can check if B is ready and expecting their move, B can show A that they are prepared. A's eyes then move to the target: this helps to ensure the accuracy of their extension and also serves to tell B where A is about to go. It is a wordless dialogue, an unspoken conversation and *it prevents accidents.*

The Sequence of Events – The attack comes first – the action. Second, the parry – the reaction. Following a successful parry, the attack has failed: A's arm is extended safely – now useless – out in the green zone and their own red zone is wide open, A is exposed – A must recover. Once A has recovered, B must improve their defensive position by resuming their own on guard position, so B then recovers.

The Dialogue – you must tell the story of this piece of stage combat. If the participants are unclear of the storyline they cannot tell it to the audience: this is a

Distance – Defining & Checking

fundamental fail for an actor. Another way of transcribing the exercise could be:

1. A – (*Locking eyes with B*) Hi! Are you ready?
2. B – (*Unwavering, looking A straight back in the eye*) Hi! Yes, I am ready.
3. A – I'm going to extend to your one section. (*Moves eyes to fix on A's non-sword hip*)
4. B – Perfectly all right, old chap! (*Drifts point out to sword side to clear way as well as signifying that not only are they ready but they know exactly where the attack is going.*)
5. A – (*On noting that B's point is adrift and A is invited in*) Hah! (*Extends, on target, out of distance, bang on the red zone of B*)
6. B – (*On allowing the extension and happy because the point is safely out of distance – and therefore does not have to rush the next bit*) Ha-hah!! (*Parries 1 by following the proscribed path, gently meeting A's foible with own forté and softly moving said item directly off target to non-sword side green zone*)
7. A – (*Having allowed their point to be moved and not having moved it themselves, now realizes that their sword is off target and their attack has failed by being successfully parried*) Dash it! (*Thinks.*) Best regroup and plan my next move before B strikes me while I am vulnerable, what with my sword extended and directed harmlessly out of danger. (*Recovers*)
8. B – (*Watching as A withdraws their sword from its offensive position and returning to the relatively non-dangerous status of on guard, and thinking that their own sword now is occupying a*

Distance – Defining & Checking

somewhat redundant position, as it is vertical and not really ready for any counter-attack or indeed making any other parry, recovers.)

This will eventually progress to resemble something more like the following – but please do not run before you are on balance, never mind walking…

1. A "You evil swine! I will run you through! Take that!" (*Thrusts*)
2. B "You think you can kill me with that pathetic move? I am the best swordsman in all of France! Watch this and learn, Pig!" (*Parries*)
3. A "Oh woe! My attack has failed. And I am exposed – I need to regroup and consider my next move before it is too late!" (*Recovers*)
4. B "And now…" (*Recovers*) "…it is my turn!"

And this is what turns a sequence of technical moves into a living, breathing struggle for life or death between two adversaries we have feelings about. And it begins, at this stage, by getting the events in the correct sequence and understanding why it is correct.

(Another – equally valid – interpretation at this stage is that 'any exchange is a giving and acknowledging of permissions': A asks for permission to extend, B gives it by opening the target and inviting the thrust, A thanks B by thrusting on target and out of distance, thereby inviting B to Parry under no pressure; B reciprocates by parrying, A allows themselves to be parried (not doing the parry for

Distance – Defining & Checking

B), B waits for A to recover, A does so and in doing so invites B to recover in turn. A very gentlemanly arrangement!)

This exercise should be repeated to each of the other three guards and then reversed (B becomes the attacker, A the defender). *Please note: when reversing this – or most exercises – it is not necessary to physically change sides…*

When confident with this, then alternate attacker/defender roles with this exercise:

1. A – Extend One
2. B – Parry 1
3. A – Recover
4. B – Recover
5. B – Extend One
6. A – Parry 1
7. B – Recover
8. A – Recover
9. A – Extend Two
10. B – Parry 2
11. ….etc.

Extend & Lunge, Parry, Recover

Once mastery of the last exercise has been achieved you will be ready to move on by adding the lunge. Make sure that you are fluent with the required fingerwork and parry positions before you tackle this one as it soon palls if you have to remain in a full lunge for five minutes while your partner patiently tries to remember the path to parry 1…

Distance – Defining & Checking

Remember, too, not to corrupt your lunge by leaning forward or overstepping with the front foot, both of which are all too tempting as you add an extended sword and a target into the lunge mix. The difference of alignment to high or low line targets is made with the sword arm and sword, not the body.

Remember: Eye-contact, the Sequence of Events and the Dialogue. *NOTE: the Sequence of Events is not the same as the Running Order – the latter refers to the order in which the moves come (thrust to one which is parried one, then a thrust to two which is parried two etc.), while the former refers to the order in which the parts of each move occur.*

One vitally important difference now is that the shift of the eyes to the target, whilst simultaneously extending, constitutes the first request, and the drift of the defender's point opens the way for the lunge.

To presume an element of psychological realism here: the exercise is broken down into units with objectives, tactics, obstacles and a super-objective. Shock! Horror! Stage Combat is Acting… what ultimately makes a fight scene such a challenge is that the units are tiny, the objectives intense, the stakes are the highest and the time it all happens in is very, very short.

CUTS – ATTACKS WITH EDGE

Making a Cut

The most spectacular bits of the swordfight – the flurry of cuts made while attacking the hapless opponent…

How do we make them safely?

Ever thrown a dart? Or a Frisbee? Or a paper aircraft? Yes? Then you can make safe cuts.

This is a continuation from the sections on 'Footwork' and 'On Guard'.

You are going to attack your opponent's right bicep with a cut. Assuming you are correctly gripping a sword with a single cutting edge, then the attack is led with the four finger knuckles and guided with the thumb behind the grip.

On guard, with your blade extended in front of you, your hand pronated, drop the point of your sword, draw your hand across your chest, level with your bicep, parallel to the floor and raise your point so that your forearm and blade are aligned: your thumb should finish just touching your own left upper arm, midway down. You have now coiled yourself like a spring, ready to unleash the attack on your unsuspecting victim…except that this has been carefully rehearsed.

Cuts – Attacks With Edge

Now slowly uncoil your arm starting from the shoulder, then the elbow, the wrist and finally the fingers until your sword is fully extended and pointing beyond your partner some 20 – 30cms to their right – your left – i.e. AWAY from their body.

From this position – and the feeling is that a laser light is being projected from the tip of your sword into the distance beyond your partner in a straight line from your right shoulder through your arm and along your blade – reverse the movement, withdrawing your blade along the same line until your thumb is again adjacent to your bicep. From here, allow the point of your sword to drop and sweep across the floor as you recover back to your original on guard position.

Assuming you are facing a right-handed partner, this cut of 3 (or cut of 4 against a leftie) is the most natural cut to make and equates to the backhand in tennis. Or throwing a paper dart past your partner's right side. Or a Frisbee. The feeling is that the energy of your move is being directed *beyond* your partner, not *into* your partner as it would be if you were completing a circle or an arc with your blade.

This action can also be likened to the flicking movement of a fly-fisher. With your partner on the receiving end and meeting your attack with either parry 3 or parry 4 (depending on whether they are left or right handed) the resultant sound should be a ringing 'chink' of metal lightly

Cuts – Attacks With Edge

glancing off metal, not the dull 'thunk' of metal driving *into* metal, like a hammer hitting a nail.

Practice this cut until it is smooth, flowing, and gentle and bears no trace of impact. Your partner should be able to use their forefinger to make the parry and feel no pain.

Now try the cut to 2 (1 if your partner is a leftie). Exactly the same prep except that your thumb only has to touch your left hip – The recurring theme is that the cut is prepared in the same line as the attack –

- attack the bicep = prep at bicep level;
- attack hip = prep at hip level.

Apart from economy & clarity of movement, it tells your partner where you are going to strike. Useful for the defender...

Now for the forehand: Exactly the same but on the other side and it feels a lot more awkward. Start with a cut to 1 (2 if your partner is leftie). Drop your point down to your right side and prep the attack as far behind you as you can, keeping the wrist below the elbow. Your hand will be supinated, you will lead with the second knuckles and your thumb will be behind it all. Now the energy (the laser) is directed past your partner by the thumb. Again, recovery is via the line of preparation and attack.

Cuts – Attacks With Edge

The cut to 4 (3 if leftie) is prepped the same way as the cut to 1 except that having dropped the point from the on guard position, you allow the sword hand to swing back and rise above the elbow until it is nearly at shoulder height. From there, cast your attack beyond your partner at bicep height and recover back the way you came.

Head Parries

The cut to the head is a vertical attack aimed at the centre of the head – right between the eyes! Up until now, all cuts have been lateral attacks met with vertical parries; this vertical attack is met with a lateral parry. There are two options open to us here, both of which protect the target with the forté when positioned correctly.

The parry 5 position has the sword held above the head, blade parallel to the ground, arm straight and pushed upwards and forwards to an angle of approximately 45° from your shoulder. (*Shortening the Arm: Straighten either arm in front of you, keeping it parallel to the ground. Note how far in front of your body your hand is – an entire arm's length! Raise the arm until it is vertical. While your hand is still an arm's length away from your body it is not IN FRONT – i.e. between you and your partner: the 'length' - or 'reach' - of the arm has been shortened to zero. Remembering that your partner is working out of distance and therefore the cut will not reach you, neither will it reach your parry, thereby creating the very real danger of the point dropping down into the face. You must push the arm up*

Cuts – Attacks With Edge

*and as **far forward as possible** without the blade exposing the top of your head.)*

Parry 5a is like a mirror image of parry 5 with the sword hand on the non-sword side of the head. This is a spectacular and glamorous element of stage sword-slinging but obviously susceptible to peril. I make no apology for repeating the same warnings in slightly different ways in the following paragraphs, however, you must, gentle reader, appreciate the safety concerns involved when directing armed attacks to the head.

The Path to Parry 5
1. Drift the point out to the sword side.
2. Drop the point towards the floor and continue in this line until the blade is parallel to the floor, sword hand on sword Side, point aiming to non-sword side.
3. Draw the hand up alongside the body, the forté of the horizontal blade passing up in front of your face. Meet and make safe the blade.
4. Following the recovery of the attacker, recover back the way you came.

The Path to Parry 5a
1. Drift the point out to the sword side.
2. Pull the hilt, pommel first, across the front of the thighs until the blade is parallel to the floor, sword hand on son-sword side, point aiming to sword side.
3. Draw the hand up alongside the body, the forté of the horizontal blade passing up in front of your face. Meet and make safe the blade

Cuts – Attacks With Edge

4. Following the recovery of the attacker, recover back the way you came.

5 & 5a: Plenty of potential for hazard…

Check out parries 3 & 4 again. Move your arm across your body from one to the other and back again and you should see that your elbow stays the same distance in front (i.e. between you and your attacker) of your body. Same deal with 2 & 1. Now assume third guard; watch your elbow as you slowly raise your arm up to parry 5. As soon as you start to raise your arm the elbow begins to get closer to you. It must do, as when your arm is vertical your elbow is next to your head. If you watch your sword, you will see that the blade moves closer to you as you raise your arm. You are out of distance; your opponent's blade will be stopping/falling short of your actual position; if your parry 5 is built on a vertical arm you will be short of connecting with the attacking blade which means it runs the real risk of dropping down into your face…

Pushing the arm further out in front of you will cause the blade to lower (the arm being hinged at the shoulder) ultimately exposing the top of your head.

As a guide, use your peripheral vision. With your eyes holding eye-contact you're your partner (real or imagined) raise your hand until it is just on the edge of this field of sight. Above all, ensure that you are not looking at your attacker OVER the horizontal parry you are attempting…

Cuts – Attacks With Edge

Same rule applies to 5a, however, this is a little trickier because the arm is bent and twisted – it is very easy to drop this parry to a too-low position and, equally, it is all too tempting to straighten the arm too much, which means that are looking at your attacker on the wrong side of your parrying arm (this arm now being on the sword side of your head and not where it should be, the non-sword side). If you look straight up now you will see that there is no blade above your head, merely fresh air.

The main concern with less than perfect head parries is that two things can (and do) happen:

1. The attacker overstretches their lunge to connect with the parry, thus closing the distance to in distance;
2. The defender leans – or even steps – forwards to find the cutting blade with their parry – again bringing both to in distance.

Head Cuts

From the on guard position you have the choice to drop the point down either to your sword, or non-sword, side and then sweep it up in a large circle to the target. Whichever side, you will keep your blade as close to your body as possible until it is over your head and able to take a vertical trajectory down towards the centre of your partner's skull. The point at which your blade passes through vertical when it is overhead is the point at which the trajectory changes and the blade behaves like a fly-

Cuts – Attacks With Edge

fishing rod and is flicked over and beyond your partner's head.

A note to help: stand in front of a mirror. Imagine a force field extending from your body around your image, 20 – 30cms outside the image. Or imagine your partner's big sibling who is 20 – 30cms higher and broader standing directly behind your partner.

This is your target. Or rather, this is your wall – a wall which you cannot breach. The favourite analogy here is to fly-fishing and that you are attempting to cast over the wall to a river beyond. An important note here is that the cut must be lined up with the centre of the head – right between the eyes. This precise targeting is vital partly for verisimilitude in the eyes of the audience but chiefly so that the defender knows exactly where to place their parry.

Unarmed 2 – Reversal of Energy

Reversal of Energy

Stage combat is illusion: two people working together to convince a third party that they are seeing something they are not. This is most easily demonstrated in this first section which deals with reversal of energy – doing the opposite of what you would do in real life.

Strangling

This starts with two people, facing each other. 1 grabs 2 with both hands around the throat and commences to choke the life out of them.

How do we create the illusion?

Well, in real life 1 would be trying their utmost to squash their hands together in order to compress 2's throat. Under reversal of energy (RofE) rules, 1 actually takes their hands, gently but firmly, AWAY from 2's neck.

How do we make this look real? After all, pulling your hands away from someone's throat is not going to convince any audience that they are witnesses to an attempted murder.

A natural reaction for 2 would be – in real life – to grab 1's wrists and attempt to pull the offending hands from their own throat. RofE rules state the opposite, so while 1 is doing their best to take their hands away from 2's throat, 2

Unarmed 2 – Reversal of Energy

is actually holding 1's wrists and pulling 1's hands onto their own neck – strangling themselves.

This simple but very effective illusion works only if both parties play their part, i.e. looking to the audience as if they really are doing what they want the audience to believe they are doing, whilst in *reality* they are doing the opposite.

There is an inbuilt safety to this trick: 2 is totally in control of what happens to their neck – if they don't like it, they simply let go of 1's wrists, and 1's hands, because of the reversal, automatically spring away from the vulnerable neck/throat area.

So here is a primary safety – ***Victim Control***.

Exercise:

Before we go any further, it is important to cover and understand the following exercise and its implications in the world of RofE, and clarify further exactly what is meant by 'victim control'.

Once both participants are in position and ready to start, the first thing that happens is eye-contact.

Eye-contact is the most important of the primary safeties in stage combat and I make no apology for repeating an earlier paragraph from this Handbook:

Unarmed 2 – Reversal of Energy

*"**Eye-contact** – the first, last and everything-in-between safety of Stage Combat. A look conveys a thousand words. A can check if B is ready and expecting their move, B can show A that they are prepared etc. A's eyes the move to the target: this helps to ensure accuracy of Extension and also serves to tell B where A is about to go. It is a wordless dialogue, an unspoken conversation and it prevents accidents."*

In this instance, both participants can inhabit their own little worlds whilst preparing, however, as soon as contact is about to be made the exercise is all about two people working as one. It is also about safety…

Victim stands with their arms at their sides; raise the hands so that they are at chest height *without moving the elbows*. Now lock the elbows in place by pushing them into the sides of the body. At no time during this exercise should the elbows – or the inside of the upper arms - lose contact with the body.

Aggressor now offers one of their wrists so that it can easily be gripped by both of the victim's hands. The aggressor is now ready to move the victim to a new position.

Make sure that you are following this as it appears 'back-to-front'. Aggressor has prepped and offered their wrist and victim has prepped and gripped this wrist with both of their hands, elbows locked into the sides of their body: the eyes now meet and the visual check for readiness is made.

Unarmed 2 – Reversal of Energy

When the aggressor is satisfied and certain that the victim is ready to move, aggressor will break eye-contact and look away…to the spot into which they are going to place their partner.

This is a secondary safety. The set/location will be familiar and all moves carefully choreographed and meticulously rehearsed, however, it is always wise to adopt a 'belt-and-braces' approach. For an accident to happen, two things have to go wrong at the same time. The 'belt-and-braces' approach teaches us to build in three safeties to every move so that even if two safeties fail, there is always a third to prevent mishaps. In this case, aggressor is performing a final check to make sure that the space into which they are moving the victim is clear for that purpose. Eyes remain on that space until the move is complete, at which point eye-contact is restored for the next moment. Beware - instinct will make you want to watch your partner as you move them. Fight this instinct: once you have checked that they are ready, they remain glued to your arms – you *know* where they are, you control where they are going, therefore it is *you* who must make sure that their destination is safe.

Aggressor now gently moves their arm sideways and away from the victim. Let us say that the aggressor is using their right arm, simply move the arm to the right until it is nearly fully extended to their right side. *Note: the arm remains relaxed at all times – it is not a rod of iron muscle, rather a soft noodle…'noodle-arm'..!* With their elbows locked into their

Unarmed 2 – Reversal of Energy

body, the victim has to be led by the aggressor's arm and allow themselves to follow it. Aggressor should only move their arm as far as they can before they have to move their feet; victim should remain passive and follow where they are led without pre-empting the move. The victim should only have to move one or two steps. At the end of this move, victim will have come to a stop after a couple of steps to their left, and aggressor will have only moved their arm. The victim follows, and must not 'do the work', pre-empt or add any energy on top of that which the aggressor has given them. This will manifest itself as an extra half-step or step, which will off-balance the aggressor, causing them to move their feet or fall. Pulling your partner off-balance is unsafe and must be avoided. Both participants must start, move and end on-balance.

Practise this a few times to make sure that everything that needs to happen happens and in the right order:

1. Eye-contact
2. Victim & aggressor prep and engage;
3. Eye-contact is resumed – readiness check is done;
4. Aggressor breaks eye-contact to check space;
5. Aggressor gently starts to lead victim;
6. Victim follows;
7. Aggressor stops leading;
8. Victim stops following;
9. Eye-contact resumed.

Unarmed 2 – Reversal of Energy

When both participants are satisfied that everything is in place then the victim can add the next ingredient – an illusion of lack of control. This is done by not moving the feet immediately the aggressor begins to pull their arm. Remember, the elbows must remain locked into the sides of the body, so the victim has to allow their body to start leaning into the pull, leaving the feet behind, until they reach the point of loss of balance. Now they allow their feet to move, 'catching up' with the body. The illusion of being off-balance.

Two faults can creep in at this stage and they must be watched for:

1 – The victim allows their elbows to leave their sides and their arms to straighten. This causes a 'bungee' effect and will throw the victim well beyond the limits of balance and control, taking the aggressor with them;

2 – The victim tries to heighten the effect by throwing themselves into the 'catching-up' element of the move, again which will accelerate them beyond the limits of control and safety, again taking the aggressor with them

Beware: any tiniest hint of the victim adding energy to this move during the previous stage will be amplified at this stage, with the result that aggressor will be pulled off-balance and out of control.

Unarmed 2 – Reversal of Energy

If any problems are encountered at any time by either or both participants, go back a stage, review and rehearse: *build slowly – never, ever go for speed.*

Assuming that all is well then the next stage can be added. From position 'a', aggressor has led victim to position 'b'. By moving their arm from right to left, aggressor can lead victim back to 'a', or through 'a' to a third position 'c'.

Same rules: eye-contact has been resumed at the end of the first move: aggressor & victim have checked that the other is OK; both now check that the other is ready for the next move ('b' to 'c').

Part of this check is to ensure that victim is physically set-up so that they will lead forwards to their next destination. The natural movement for the victim here is to describe an arc around the aggressor and keeping their face/front towards them. Beware that if the victim has turned to face their left then any movement in the opposite direction will push them backwards instead of leading them forwards. Use the ending of the first move to set up for the start of the second.

By this stage we should have an illusion of the aggressor pulling the victim from side to side while the victim almost falls off-balance and just manages to stay on their feet.

Aggressor can now make this look more, well, aggressive by using their body and their voice to add to the illusion of violence with appropriate movement, tension and sound. However, whatever the aggressor adds to the rest of their movement, it *stops at the shoulder of the working arm* which remains in noodle-arm state throughout.

So much for the exercise, what is its application? Well, if the aggressor, instead of having their working hand unconnected to anything and just waving in the breeze, were to connect to a part of the victim's body, it is possible to start creating some great illusions:

Hair Pull

Aggressor: spread the fingers of the working hand; place it on the head of your victim; now gently curl the fingers and thumb into a loose claw – do not ball it into a fist – and rest the first knuckle/fingernails against the victim's scalp. (*For the sake of this Handbook, we number the knuckles from the fingertip down: move down the finger from its tip; just past the nail is the first knuckle; the middle finger section leads to the second knuckle, and the third knuckle is the big, punching knuckle, where the finger joins the hand.*)

Tufts of hair should stick out through the gaps between the fingers but none of it is actually held. Test this by maintaining the claw shape and gently lifting the hand away from the head, letting the hair fall back into place. No hair is actually held, however, with tufts sticking out, it *looks* as though it is.

Unarmed 2 – Reversal of Energy

Victim now grips the working wrist of the aggressor with both of their hands and locks in their elbows (the body will have to bend a little to facilitate this). Aggressor can again lead victim from side to side with their hands – exactly as in the exercise, however, with the appearance of gripping hair, we can create the illusion that the victim's hair is being held and that they are being pulled around by it.

Clarification: we have gone through the exercise and we have applied it to form an illusion. But we have blurred the parameters of 'victim control'…haven't we..?

This is true – in this case it is the aggressor who is doing the pulling and the victim who is being pulled. This is 'real' not 'stage' fighting, surely?

And didn't we just say that the rules of RofE state that in stage combat we do the *opposite* of what we do in real life?

Again, true. But think of this: if at any time the victim doesn't like or know or want to join in with anything being offered by the aggressor, then all they have to do is release the aggressor's wrists. Because the aggressor is not really holding any hair – they are not holding anything other than a position – the move immediately, and safely, stops. Thus, the victim has ultimate control.

One argument is that it should be the victim who throws themselves around and the aggressor simply acts the aggression. In practise, it is very difficult for this not to

Unarmed 2 – Reversal of Energy

look like what it is, a 'victim' throwing themselves around, as the 'aggressor' is a beat or so behind the victim's movements which jars visually.

Also, in the hair pull position, the victim's eyes are directed down to the stage/floor; it is the aggressor who is free to look around and ensure that the victim doesn't collide into anything or anyone.

So, both visually and from a safety aspect it is more effective for there to be an element of aggressor control, however, ultimate control must lie with the victim.

TRANSITIONS

At this point it should be stated that the moves themselves are not difficult and with only a small amount of practice most *people* are able to do them effectively. As previously mentioned, stage combat can only exist within a context – believable characters in a situation where words have failed and the only recourse is physical violence. And this is what requires an *actor*.

Actors can view stage fighting as the least 'method' or 'system' approach – it is repetitive, technical and uncreative. This completely erroneous take on the subject usually stems from the fact that it is the least practiced of all the actor's skills…they forget how many years of practice they have had at walking and breathing for these things to be second nature! No matter how naturally gifted a dancer is, they still must *learn* the repertoire of moves before they can interpret them creatively within any choreography.

Once you get to the stage of not having to think of all the safeties and techniques because they are as instinctive and natural as your mother tongue, then creativity can be unleashed with all the passion and commitment needed in a scene of physical conflict.

At the top here I stated that the moves are not difficult – they are not. Nor are they the most important part of a fight scene. The acting is. And acting is what must happen

Transitions

throughout the scene, irrespective of the props and physicality.

For example, in the middle of a heated argument between two characters, at the point where one of them finally gives in to the animalistic, primeval urge to damage the other by going for their throat, it just doesn't work for the actors to drop out of character, get their hands in the right place, check that they are both OK, and then suddenly resume the scene…

So how do we escalate smoothly into violence? And once there, how does one thing lead to another?

We now look a little bit at the most important part of choreography and acting ability, the transitions. Transitions are the parts that make or break a fight scene.

Getting into the strangle

Obviously it would be potentially extremely dangerous for one actor to launch themselves at the other's throat in the heat of intense emotion, but we can create the *effect* safely, with a little thought and a bit of rehearsal…

Show & Go

So we have the context:

A: You swine!
B: You pig!
A: I will kill you..!

Transitions

(A then lunges at B and strangles them)
The transition from words to action follows thus:

A and B are two steps apart.

A: Raises their hands in an 'I surrender' pose and leans backwards a little; this shows their intention to the audience, but more importantly *offers a cue to B.*

B acknowledges the cue via the medium of eye-contact *(through the eyes, A asks B if they are ready and B replies that they are ready and prepared.)*

A takes two steps forward. On the second step, A is within arm's reach of B.

A extends their hands forward and places them on B's shoulders.

A takes a third step forward as B takes a step backwards *(to give the illusion that A has pushed B backwards).*

During this third step, B takes A's wrists with their hands and guides A's hands to their (B's) throat into the strangle position.

As soon as A's wrists are grabbed, A begins the reversal of energy and starts to pull away, meantime, B has already instigated their own reversal and is pulling the strangle into their own throat.

Transitions

Where it goes from there depends upon the choreography but *a fight only works with believable transitions…*

Unarmed 3 - More Examples of RofE

Arguably the simplest trick in the book, RofE is incredibly versatile and the number of applications and variations are multitudinous, limited only by how warped, twisted and depraved the imagination is…

Finger Squeeze

Aggressor stands in 'bodybuilder' pose, arms bent and the hands at waist height with fingers touching first and second knuckles. Touch the tips of the forefingers with tips of the thumbs and you have made two holes for the victim's fore and middle fingers of one hand. They insert their fingers, aggressor suddenly flexes their arm muscles, pushing their hands into each other whilst maintaining the looseness of the 'holes', and emits a roar; victim reacts with all of their body except their working hand (which can be retracted at any time owing to the fact that it is not actually being held), and screams.

Pure RofE – nothing is happening but the audience sees/hears an action, sees/hears a reaction and two plus two now equals five!

Interlocked Finger Wrestle

Classic wrestler battle: aggressor and victim stand opposite each other, raise their hands as if in surrender, spread their fingers and then engage. All muscles except those of the hands are then tensed and the victim makes a great play of bending over backwards, as if being forced, while the aggressor merely acts. The roles of victim and aggressor may be reversed any number of times to create a story.

Nose Pull

As the hair pull but the aggressor raises hand in a 'peace sign', curls fore and middle finger and offers up the first and second knuckles of both fingers to the victim's face, either side of their nose. Aggressor must remember to always keep forcing their fingers apart as the most common fault here is to *actually* squeeze. Which isn't so good if the victim happens to have a cold…

Ear Pull

As with the hair pull but this time the working hand is cupped and the row of first knuckles is offered to the side of the victim's head just behind their ear. The heel of the aggressor's hand rests on the victim's face just in front of the ear while the ear itself does not need to be touched, much less actually held.

NOTE: Hair, nose, ears etc. – the pain comes from trying to separate them from the body…as you learn these moves double-check yourself that you are not actually looking like you are trying to push these parts of the body more firmly into place…and for the victim, ensure that your reaction reinforces the illusion: if your hair is being pulled it is followed by the piece of scalp to which it is attached. Try gently pulling a strand of your own hair to see. Also gently tug your ear or tweak your nose. Now as you play your part in the illusions, focus on pushing the pulled bit into the aggressor's hand.

Unarmed 3 - More Examples of RofE

Also, importantly, this stuff does not require any element of speed, in fact on most occasions, slowly and deliberately is more effective.

Testicle Grab

Anything aggressive towards the sexual organs is helped by the fact that audiences, being human, have a car crash mentality that really wants to see someone get kicked in the nuts...

Aggressor makes a claw of their working hand (making it at eye level whilst staring into the victim's eyes can work well). Place the claw over the victim's groin. Victim grips wrist – do not obscure the claw. Aggressor simply pulses tension through their body (not the claw) and victim squeals correspondingly.

To finish, aggressor dips their shoulder, victim releases their grip on the wrist and flattens their hands. Aggressor flattens the claw hand and pushes the back of it into the palms of the victim. The hand is then pulled away at speed and the victim screams, pulls their knees together and slowly lowers themselves to the floor.

Nipple Tweak

Make a loose fist and push the pad of the thumb onto the side of the second forefinger knuckle. Simply offer this to the victim's nipple and keeping the hand gripped, sharply twist the hand through ninety degrees. Works very well when done with both hands...

Unarmed 3 - More Examples of RofE

Fishhook

This is either one or both forefingers 'hooked' into the corner(s) of the victim's mouth. One finger can be done from the side and two from behind. Aggressor must keep fingers locked in position and allow the victim to manoeuvre them.

Headlock

This is the classic 'head-under-the-armpit' move! The trick here is for the aggressor to make a 'circle of energy' with their arms to form a hole through which the victim inserts their head. The circle of energy is tension created by the aggressor and directed into the aggressor. It gives a muscular dynamic which creates the illusion of pressure. For example, to apply the headlock with the left hand: cross the right arm over the body so the little finger rests on the left hip and the hand open. Clench the left fist and place it into the right palm – the left elbow will be way out to the side - and there will be the hole for the head. An alternate grip is to place the thumb of the right hand against the left hip so that the open palm faces downwards. The left fist/wrist is now placed into the palm of the right hand. Left hand pushes up and the right pushes down to generate the circle of energy. The victim now slips their head through the hole and controls the aggressors left arm with their hands, holding either just the left forearm, or the left elbow and forearm, or left hand on the forearm or elbow and right hand around aggressor's waist. All these choices depend as much on personal taste as choreography – there is no right or wrong, only what is safe and works…

Whichever grip you may choose, it is possible for the aggressor to pull the victim around by the 'head' (in reality the hands) in quite a vicious manner, even off their feet.

Arm Lock – Arrest

This is the arm lock where the arm is held straight and out to the side and the hand is rotated (in real life) so as to cause the body to bend over forwards. That is, if the victim's arm is held out to the side with the palm facing forwards and the thumb uppermost, the hand turns so that the thumb rotates forward and towards the ground, at which point the body starts to bend and the hand finishes palm up.

The victim does everything, twisting their own arm and body and contorting with pain. The aggressor acts the action while connecting with the victim only with a light, easily broken grip.

Arm Lock – Half Nelson

As above, the victim does the work; the aggressor only has to act. This move has the victim's arm forced downwards, twisted behind their back and with the back of their hand on their back, the arm is 'forced' upwards. There is an element of pure RofE in this move but as it is much easier the aggressor to push the arm down than for the victim to push upwards against it then we have to compromise.

Unarmed 3 - More Examples of RofE

While the strangle may be viewed – and learned – as 100% RofE, i.e. 50/50 effort ratio split between aggressor and victim, the Half Nelson is probably 80/20 or even 90/10. Similarly some actors are stronger than others and while a technique may be 100% RofE it may not require 100% of that actor's muscle power.

Strangle from Behind

Aggressor stands behind the victim, stomach pressed into their back so that there is no gap. (Gaps allow for impact and impact is the road to pain). To strangle with the right arm, extend the right arm straight over the victim's right shoulder and move the body to the left enough to locate your head above and behind their right shoulder. Victim then takes hold of the straight, right arm at the wrist and the elbow, and bends it around their throat. As the bending commences so the RofE begins until the strangle is in place, the victim pushing the arm into their own throat and the aggressor is pushing the arm away from the throat.

Lifted Strangle Against a Wall

This comes from the strangle from the front described above except this time the victim is backed against a wall. Victim bends knees and jumps vertically while the aggressor readjusts their feet (usually by stretching one foot backwards) to drop underneath the victim whilst straightening their arms. Aggressor is braced by their back leg and leaning at an angle into the wall. Victim is hanging on the aggressor's wrists by their hands (you will have tested that the victim can support their own weight first…).

Ditto with Props

Variation on the above involves using a pool cue or baseball bat or length of steel pipe etc. with the victim hanging from the prop by their hands and resting their throat on the bar. Performed with two aggressors it may be possible to raise the victim slowly off their feet.

Leg Lock

See notes above on arm locks – classic wrestling leg lock involves the victim lying face down with the aggressor kneeling on the back of their thigh, their knee bent and the upraised foot being 'unscrewed' from the ankle. Actually, the aggressor carefully places the toes and knee so that the victim's thigh is covered by the gap under the aggressor's ankle. The victim's foot is clasped to the chest of the aggressor and held still while the aggressor winds up and twists his shoulders…again, an action, a reaction and a result adding up to five!

Finger Lock

Twisted, pushed or bent, it is apparently possible to exercise maximum control with minimum effort…at this point you should be able to figure these moves out – use your own imagination, gentle reader!

Unarmed 3 - More Examples of RofE

Rope Pull

A rope is tied around the victim's waist and they are dragged around by it. In actuality, the rope is 'tied' with a thread or a release knot. The victim holds onto the rope as it trails away from their body. The short length of rope between their body and their hands is kept slack by the grip. The tension is only on the length of rope running from the victim's hands to those of the aggressor.

Caveman Drag

Variation on the rope pull in which the long-haired victim gathers a short length of slack hair and holds it tight to their scalp while the aggressor takes hold of the end of the rest of it and pulls the victim using this short, natural tow-rope. The victim can be pulled along the ground on their back, assisting by pushing themselves along with their feet in the guise of struggling. As above, the actual pulling is done with and to the hands.

Pulling & Pushing

While it is well-nigh impossible to inflict 'whiplash'-style injuries to yourself by turning and twisting, it is surprisingly easy to injure another person with even the slightest of shoves if they are not expecting it, or there is more force behind it than anticipated.

To pull someone around to face you: place your hand on their shoulder. They can then act being pulled around and you only have to act the pulling.

Unarmed 3 - More Examples of RofE

Similarly with pushing and shoving – place the hand(s) on the victim's shoulder(s) and direct any energy over and beyond the shoulder(s) while they perform the push.

The above examples are by no means exhaustive! There are many variations and applications reversal of energy…experiment and add to this list!

Unarmed 4 - Intro to Impact Moves

Elbow Attack to Stomach.

To learn this technique, stand with your back pressed against a smooth wall. Raise your elbowing arm so that the hand is above your head some forty-five degrees between vertical and horizontal, and on a diagonal some forty-five degrees between straight out in front of you and out to your side. Have the palm up (supinated) and close the fist. You should be able to draw your elbow in to your waist in a straight line. Contact is with the upper half of the ribs and the fleshy inside of the upper arm – not with the point of the elbow and the hip bone (although this is possible if you allow your body to bend forward slightly – so don't bend!).

Now, move your arm fairly slowly up to the start position (all the 45's), clench fist, and draw the elbow into your side a little faster.

As you build the pace you will find that the arm will naturally bounce away from the body after contact - allow it to do so.

At no time should your elbow come into contact with the wall you are propped up against…

When you are happy that you have all the ingredients - and in the right order – then move away from the wall, and ask your partner if they will be the wall. Have them stand

Unarmed 4 - Intro to Impact Moves

behind you and slightly to the side. Their stomach should be visible to an audience watching from in front of you, at the side of your body corresponding with your attacking elbow.

Gently repeat the build up to this move as practiced against the wall until you are up to speed and absolutely not contacting your partner – all contact being directed into yourself.

Partner now needs to add a suitable stomach reaction, taking care to cheat slightly away from you so as not to smash their nose on your shoulder.

Next, add a reason for being in this position; for example, partner could be strangling you from behind with their forearm across your throat. Think carefully about where their arm is going to go when reacting. Also make sure that you are not bending forward as you strike with the elbow as, apart from possibly hitting your own hip with your elbow, you will be driving your hips backwards into your partner's and it is not nice attacking someone's vulnerabilities...

Note: the cheat here is that the gap between elbow and stomach is very small (and very tightly controlled as you are bringing the elbow in to a very specific part of your own body). Do not allow the gap to increase by allowing any separation between victim's stomach and aggressor's back. At best this will look unrealistic, at worse you will encourage aggressor to start 'heat-seeking' with their elbow in order to close the gap. The biggest safety in this move is that the aggressor must control and know exactly where their elbow finishes: the gap must be minimal and as the aggressor cannot see the victim, the victim must communicate physically by pushing their stomach into the aggressor's back. Physical communication: this is the important lesson in this technique. It is a technique that will be required in other ways as you progress to more advanced levels.

Remember: as ever, pre-empt things that could go wrong – after the elbow has struck, make sure the fist doesn't react up and towards victim's nose… etc.

Having practiced the stomach reaction, here are a couple of other techniques to learn which require a similar reaction…

Stomach Punch

This is a simple move (remembering that 'simple' does not mean the same as 'easy'), however, it is common for people to struggle to make it work. The reason for this lies in the technique required for the punch. The usual mistake is to do this with the arm only, which simply does not *look* powerful enough to warrant a reaction. The word 'look' is italicised because it is important to note that this is all being done for the ultimate gratification of an audience. To that end, there are many moves in stage combat which are not real, but *look* as if they are. Similarly, now is a good time to point out another obvious, but oft forgotten fact; that the reaction must equal the action. "For every action

Unarmed 4 - Intro to Impact Moves

there is an equal and opposite reaction." (Newton's third law, if I remember my schoolboy physics.) This means two things: firstly, that the size of the reaction must be as big or as small as the action which caused it – a punch from a 100kg attacker to a 50kg recipient would generate a different reaction than if the punch was done by the smaller person to the larger, even though in real life it is quite possible for a smaller person to hit harder than a bigger person – it is the audience's *perception of reality* that we play with. Secondly, the reaction must follow the same line as the attack – a punch travelling in one direction would knock the receiver over in that direction. Start with these basic truths at this stage.

So to the punch. The fist is clenched. *Note: - never, ever clench a fist with the thumb inside the fingers. If you were to punch like that for real you would possibly break your thumb. And the audience knows it is wrong. It looks wrong. So the thumb curls over the top finger knuckles.* For this stomach punch to look right you need to put your body into it, not just throw out your arm. Some water-ski jumpers wear a band around their torso which also goes over the upper part of one of their arms, presumably to prevent the thing from being ripped out of its socket with the force of being pulled onto the ramp. It pins the elbow into their side allowing the arm to only flex at the elbow. Imagine yourself fitted with a similar accoutrement and you will soon work out that to throw a punch with that hand you would have to swivel the body. Lead with the shoulder; throw the shoulder forward first, stop it abruptly and let the shock wave travel down the arm and into the fist to cause that to move forward sharply. It will stop sharply. You will also feel a recoil in the arm. If you allow it, it will cause the fist to bounce backwards slightly. The abrupt stop, followed immediately by the bounce of the recoil, combine to create the illusion of hitting something. Like a stomach.

Once you have perfected this punch, try it with a partner. Stand opposite them, face to face. Adjust the distance so that you have to take a small step forward with the non-punching foot (your left foot if you punch with your right hand) in order to place the palm of your non-punching hand on their shoulder. Don't cross their body, so your left hand goes to their right shoulder, or right hand to left. Do not grip the shoulder, just rest your palm on it. Keep the non-punching arm straight and the non-punching hand on the shoulder. Once you have taken your step do not move your back foot. The combination of hand position/straight arm/set rear foot combine to keep you out of distance. At this stage it will feel unnaturally out of distance – too far away. At this stage I will say "Better to be too safe…" Remember that not only does your partner not want you to actually hit them, but they would also rather like the freedom of space in front of them to be able to perform their reaction without fear of smashing their nose into your shoulder or face. This is also why you are not gripping their shoulder, just resting your palm on it as a marker.

Unarmed 4 - Intro to Impact Moves

Once you feel that you are competent and confident with this move, just for fun try it with your other hand…not so easy, huh?

The Box Masking Technique

As part of the reaction, the open hands can be brought up to positions either side of the punch, then flattening onto the stomach to complete the movement. Done slickly, they will form a box which will mask the gap between fist and stomach.

Here are two more techniques which involve the stomach reaction, an attack with the knee and a kick. Remember the 'sharp stop and recoil' effect mentioned above and apply that to the knee at the appropriate moment. Note here please that a lot, if not quite all techniques are transferable: do not fall into the trap of thinking that technique 'a' is only used in move 1 or that move 3 requires a different technique – techniques can be essentially the same, merely applied differently, in exactly the same way that, as an actor, you can have a hundred different ways to say the same line or even the same thought…

Knee to Stomach

To give the illusion of a knee attack to the stomach.

Victim stands with feet hip width apart – neutral open guard.

The attacker stands to their side at 90° to them. Step in to the victim on the left foot and bring the right knee up

Unarmed 4 - Intro to Impact Moves

sharply in front of their stomach, stopping it abruptly. The victim reacts appropriately.

In more detail: draw an imaginary line along the victim's toes. If the attacker is using their right knee for the attack, then they should stand to the right of the victim and approach with their left foot on the line. Get as close to the victim as possible, so the front of the attacker's left hip is pushed up against the outside of the victim's right. Attacker must not twist their hips in towards the victim or genuine contact will be made. The attacker's hands may be placed on victim's shoulder(s) both for balance and cueing purposes – but not to assist the victim in any way with their reaction. It is the sharpness with which the attacking knee stops which gives the illusion of contact. This knee should neither go beyond 90°, nor must it travel higher than the victim's hips, as this results in the knee becoming pointed and angled towards victim's sternum. Rather, the kneecap should be pushed across victim's body and out to the far side, keeping it as clear from the stomach as possible. If there is to be any contact (see below) it will be with the victim's stomach and the attacker's inner thigh.

Victim may hold one or both hands open, pronated, ready for the top of the attacker's leg, but this should not be depended on by the attacker as the means by which the knee stops. The victim may guide the attacker's leg in to their own stomach, partly to close the cheat and partly to tuck it in safely to their own body so it doesn't present a danger during the reaction. Victim should not, however, hold the leg; rather the attacker must be free to move it away at any time – important for balance/safety reasons.

A sharp exhalation from the victim, appropriate to air being rapidly forced out of the lungs, cements the illusion.

This move is primarily an up & down move, but can, with practice, be done in-the-round. Done ITR, it is usually better not to telegraph this move.

It is vitally important that this 'reversing the leg' technique is studied, learned and burned into the physical memory as all of us have a standard default kicking mode which is based on driving energy into, and through, the target. We probably don't remember learning this, but we will revert to it. Possibly because we don't use our legs for as many different things or in as many different ways as we use our arms, and are therefore not as dextrous with them. Incidentally, this may not look real (or feel real), but it will only not look real to someone who knows what they are looking at: done well, the vast majority of people will not register that it is fake; and those who think they do will be confused by the reaction they have witnessed and just as quickly correct their perception to conform to what the brain deduces. ("A man sees a unicorn…and because people know that unicorns don't exist, it quickly is reported as a horse with an arrow in its head" – adapted from Rosencrantz and Guildenstern Are Dead, by Tom Stoppard)

Kicking Technique

When kicking a football, for instance, the action will very often start from the shoulders; the body will rotate, in turn whipping the leg and, ultimately, the foot into contact with the target. This action is used to generate maximum impact at the point of contact. A similar technique is used in many martial arts to give a 'flicking' of the lower leg from the knee, generating speed and momentum to deliver maximum power at contact.

Basic stage combat kicking technique requires the opposite result: that minimum power is delivered by the foot at the moment of contact. This very simple theory is one of the hardest to physically master simply because it is very unnatural. But it is also this unnatural quality that makes it hard for the audience to detect the trick – even when it is telegraphed and delivered blatantly: it is not spotted because it is not encountered anywhere else.

To imagine this technique: think of standing in front of a table and slowly raising a straight leg in front of you, toes pointed so that the instep is the first part of the foot to make contact with the underside of the table. At exactly this split-second of contact imagine the lower leg dropping from the knee joint while the upper leg carries on rising. This takes the 'sting' completely out of the contact, pulling the energy away from the table instead of 'flicking' in to it.

Unarmed 4 - Intro to Impact Moves

To try this out, get your partner to kneel up (i.e. not sitting back on their heels) and hold out a cupped hand, palm down, fingers & thumb together. If kicking with the right leg, stand to your partner's right, your left foot in line with their knees, and kick into their left hand. (This is a good habit to get into for reasons which will become clearer later.) Start off by swinging your straight leg slowly and gently and 'breaking' at the knee on contact. Make sure that there is no twisting of the body in towards your partner and that you remain at right angles to them. Check with your partner that they are feeling no power transferring through the foot into their hand. As you practice you can increase the swing and pace of the move, even flowing into it with a couple of steps. Ensure that there is no change in technique as the rate increases and no reversion to 'flicking'. Partner should find that there is no impact into their hand; the hand should not fly away on contact, nor should it 'slap' down onto the incoming foot. It should be held firmly – but not rigidly - and trust in the technique. Not only should there be no pain, but you should also notice a satisfying 'whump' sound on contact which suggests to an audience that it should hurt.

Perhaps I should have mentioned at the start that this is much more comfortable for both parties if the kicking foot is shod – barefoot really stings…

Kick to Stomach
First master the basic stage combat kicking technique.

Unarmed 4 - Intro to Impact Moves

Now get your partner to stand in a neutral On Guard position. If you are kicking with the right foot, stand to their right and at 90° so that you are facing their right side. Victim brings their left hand up in front of their stomach, pronated & slightly cupped, with the fingers and thumb together. Imagine that the victim's toes are on a line; step on this line with your left foot and swing your right leg up until the foot makes contact with their hand and your knee breaks.

On contact the victim performs the stomach reaction with suitable vocalisation, and the attacker replaces their foot on floor to ensure their stability.

As ever, eye-contact should be the first thing that happens. When first learning this move, the next thing to happen will be the victim placing their hand to receive the foot. The hand should be placed midway between navel and crutch and about 10cms away from the body. Further away from, rather than closer to, the body if you wish.

Attacker now looks at the hand. Your foot will go where you are looking so it is important to look at the target. It is also very reassuring for your partner that your eyes have moved down to the target. Now step in and perform the kick taking care not to twist the hips and thus turn the kick (and the toes) in towards the victim's body – the leg/foot should travel in a straight line, upwards and in front of the victim until it meets with the hand.

Unarmed 4 - Intro to Impact Moves

The hand now instantly flattens onto the stomach and is joined by the other as the victim performs their reaction. The other hand – the one nearest the kicker – can be used to ward off or deflect the leg if you think the foot is coming to close, or simply to protect the more vulnerable parts of the body if you wish. It is there as an extra safety; if the near hand was used to receive the kick, the far hand can play little or no practical role in protection.

Make sure that you are on balance at all times and the final step prior to kicking stops your body momentum from travelling towards your partner so that there is no 'drift' in to your victim during and after the kick.

This is an up & down move with the victim's back to the audience. With a lot of practice this move can become slick with the victim's hand not moving into place until just before the foot arrives, connecting, and immediately transferring to the stomach – done well, this can work in-the-round.

To give the old stomach a rest, let us look at some basic rolls and descents. One of the biggest and most constant hazards which confront the stage combatant is the floor – it is, however, a necessary evil. Best to embrace it and make it your friend as quickly and as comfortably as possible…

Rolls & Descents

This section is heavily concerned with the avoidance of self-inflicted pain: particularly from any impact. This will be a recurring theme during the course of TSCH. Impact occurs when two things collide. Take out the collision and replace it with "gentle placing" or "a smooth dissipation" and you will get a silent, painless result – this is your objective.

The secret is BALANCE. A trick you have been practicing nearly all your life, since you were months old and first realised (albeit subconsciously) that muscle power wasn't the way forward. Since that moment of enlightenment you have learnt to stand, walk, run, skip, jump, hop, pose, etc. and to do these things in different directions and while performing other actions, some simple, some complex – do I need to go on telling you how clever you are?

> *TAKE A BREAK, LOOK BACK AND SEE HOW FAR YOU HAVE COME, INSTEAD OF BEATING YOURSELF UP ABOUT ANYTHING YOU MAY BE HAVING A LITTLE DIFFICULTY WITH RIGHT NOW.*
> (Pocket philosophy, the Author.)

Rolls & Descents

Forward Roll

Imagine a line on the floor running from between your feet away from you directly forwards.

Imagine a line running down your back, from the top of the spine at the nape of the neck down to your coccyx.

Your mission, should you choose to accept it, is to lay your personal line gently and evenly on top of the one on the floor.

To achieve this:

1. Place your feet, about hip width apart, equally on either side of the ground line.
2. Take a generous step forward on one foot. (NOTE – you will be on balance until I mention otherwise...)
3. Place your hands on the ground in front of you, about shoulder width apart, equally on either side of the line.
4. Hands too far forward – the next step is impossible
5. Hands not forward enough – you will overbalance, and crash. Take care!
6. Bend the arms and allow the trailing foot to lift in the air.
7. Keep lifting the foot, tuck the chin onto the chest and place the back of the neck on the floor line.
8. This is the point of no return. Once you have the back of your neck on the ground allow the rest of the spine to follow, giving yourself to the ground. Do not 'collapse' the body. Try to maintain shape as if you are

Rolls & Descents

      rolling over a large beach ball. Please note that you do not 'lose' balance, rather you volunteer it to the ground.
9. Allow the movement to continue until you are flat on your back, or perhaps rolled up to a sitting position. Take care not to let the heels hit the ground, this hurts.

Breathing – a smooth and even exhalation from just before the actual roll until the end of the roll. If you like, try humming without change of pitch or volume or loss of sound whilst you roll.

With a little practice the preparation phase (up till the back of the neck is on the ground) will become smooth and flowing; the exit phase can be allowed to carry on with the soles of the feet being placed on the ground and the momentum of the roll taking you up to standing. Please think of all phases as being parts of one movement which need to be done in order, so as to achieve the whole.

Remember, the forward roll is the bit from when the back of the neck touches the ground up to the bit where the whole of the back has passed through contact with the floor. What happens before and after that can be adjusted and played around with for effect, but the spine *must* be looked after.

Rolls & Descents

Shoulder Roll

This is a sufficiently varied variation of a forward roll as to warrant its own category. This is because the entry point and point of no return occur earlier in the shoulder roll than the forward roll. The roll itself follows a different line along the body, and the exit contains an inherent twisting action which opens up a whole new range of possibilities. Other than that it is exactly the same…

The ground line is the same; however, the body line runs from the outside tip of one shoulder to the opposite buttock. Let us assume the right shoulder, diagonally across the back to the left buttock. (If you were to raise the right arm up the line would continue along the outside edge of the arm to the outside of the tip of the little finger.)

Stand on your line as before, step forward as before. The first critical point has just occurred: make sure that you have stepped forward on the same foot as the marked shoulder/arm/hand. In this case the right.

As the left hand is lowered to the ground to support, the right arm sweeps down in front of and slightly across the body to allow the outside of the right little finger to be placed as a guide point on the ground line; the rest of the line up the arm follows to the floor until the back of the shoulder is placed on the ground. The tricky bit with the shoulder roll is that you are committed to rolling – i.e. off

Rolls & Descents

balance – from the point at which the left hand touches the ground. As mentioned before, this point of no return is earlier than the forward roll. Just a little bit earlier, but quite enough to be scary because you appear to be entering the roll from a greater height. (Of course, if you think about it, it's nonsense, but that's sure what it seems like…)

You must allow the momentum of the roll to take you with it and trust that, having set it up correctly, it will take you to the proper place. Now, the first time that happens you will feel as if you've travelled 360° one way and 180° another all at the same – rather quick – time. This is because you have. The roll takes you from feet to feet through 360°: (Note this roll *is* feet to feet whereas the forward roll is only along the length of the spine.) At the same time, because you initiated a twisting action by going diagonally across your back, the roll finishes that off for you and you wind up facing the way you came.

Hint – this is also known as a combat roll. It is designed to protect you if you get thrown to the ground and bring you back to your feet and facing the person who just threw you so they can't sneak up and do it again.

An alternative, equally effective, method – assuming that your forward rolls are fluid and going from feet-to-feet – is to simply perform a forward roll with a slight twist: at the prep stage, stand normally, raise one foot and both arms, step forward but instead of placing the hands on either side of the floor line place them *on* the line. This is done by moving the hands so that the hand corresponding to the raised foot is below the other, the same distance apart as they would be in the side-by-side configuration. Turn both hands so that the fingers are pointing inwards: this will cause the elbows to point outwards and flex slightly. Then commit to the roll. The changed hand position creates the shoulder roll line and the rest just happens.

Curtsey Method Descent

This can be done on either side, for the sake of clarity I will take you through it on the right side.

1. Stand normally.
2. Place the ball of the right foot on the floor behind and to the left of the left foot. (As if about to curtsey).
3. Weight is evenly distributed on both feet.
4. Start bending the knees as if curtseying; continue to slowly bend the knees; continue slowly bending the knees until you can place the right knee on the floor.
5. Swivel the upper body as far as you can to the left.
6. Reach forward with the hands and lean forward from the hips to maintain balance as you
7. Slowly sit backwards onto the right buttock (keep the buttock off the floor as long as you can, and allow the right foot to slip off its ball and onto the instep/outside edge of the foot).
8. Once the right buttock has been placed on the floor, slowly roll out along the back, taking care not to let the

Rolls & Descents

head drop on the floor. Remember, tuck it into the chest.

9. If you started facing the audience when you were standing, they will now be at right angles to you, on your right, as you lay.

Big Step Descent
Begin in a comfortable standing position.

Take as large a step back with one foot as you can comfortably manage. As your weight is now nearly all on this back foot, the corresponding leg is referred to as the 'supporting leg'. So you've stepped back on your left, the left leg is the supporting leg. Clear? Good.

Now start to bend the supporting leg. As you do this, test your balancing skills for you are going to see how far you can bend this leg without losing balance. Keep the right leg (the trailing leg, if you will) straight, allow the toes to lift but keep the heel on the floor. Lean the body forward from the hips. Reach forward with the arms. If you allow the supporting knee to drift out a little, you should be able to get your left buttock to within small centimetres of the ground, close to your left heel. Lean your body a little further forward, reach your arms a little more in front of you and this will help you get a little closer to the ground. When you are as low as you can get – and it will surprise you how near to the ground that is – you will be able to place, gently, that (left) buttock on the ground without impact. From here, simply roll out along your back until you are laying down flat. Do not let the head drop on the floor – keep the chin tucked onto the chest.

Note that you are placing only one buttock – trying to place both may lead to the coccyx getting uncomfortably close to the floor first, and that can hurt.

This should be a very slow and controlled descent. Only when you are very confident and comfortable with this move should you try to get down quicker. Practice until you can do the whole thing without thinking about each of the constituent elements and can treat it as one move, instead of several moves linked together.

This is a vital part of all aspects of stage combat: the thorough learning of all of the elements, and the order in which they come, until they are done as one move, under complete control. Once that has been accomplished, and you no longer have to think about what you are doing, can you add other things, like weapons or an opponent or a performance. But these are things which are still a long way off.

Trip

Attacker pushes victim from the front while catching the back of their leg with their foot causing them apparently to lose balance and be directed to the floor.

Victim stands in a neutral on guard, Attacker facing them. Eye-contact. Attacker steps forward and to one side of the victim using the outside leg, placing their hands on the top

Rolls & Descents

of the victim's shoulders. Victim commences Big Step Descent as the attacker takes a second step forward, this time on their inside leg, and places the foot on the ground behind the victim's trailing leg. As victim falls away, completing their BS Descent the attacker acts 'pushing'.

Firstly, and rather obviously, the attacker must know which foot the victim intends to step back on – which leg is going to be their supporting leg – in order that they move to the victim's *other* side. This makes sure that the attacker is 'blocking' the leg which isn't going to move – the trailing leg. Secondly, the hand placement (resting flat on the top of the victim's shoulders) ensures that if there is any force accidentally directed towards the victim, that force will cause the attacker's hands to slide off and over the victim, *not* assist them towards the ground.

The third step the attacker makes – with the victim committed to their line of descent – will naturally take them away from the victim. This separation is helpful in avoiding the attacker treading on, or falling over/on top of the victim.

This is an in-the-round move, which features the victim doing all the work, and the attacker using timing and acting to cement the illusion.

Backward Roll

Start this by lying on the ground on your back. Draw your knees up and onto your chest. Try it again with a little

Rolls & Descents

more energy from the knees until you feel the energy causing the hips to lift from the ground. Now add the hands: as your knees pull up, place the hands, palm down, under your shoulders, fingertips pointing to your hips, fingers parallel to the spine. It is essential that you keep your elbows pointing skywards, as the distance from the ground to your elbow is the space you will create to allow your head to pass through and so not put undue pressure on the neck. Allowing your elbows to splay out away from your head brings them closer to the ground and significantly reduces the gap.

Once you are comfortable with this little sequence of events and it is all flowing smoothly, simply increase the pull on the strings to draw the knees up with more energy. Think of the strings as two pieces of elastic, and in your mind anchor the other ends first at your chest, then at your shoulders and then to the ground above your shoulders at the side of your ears. When the elastic finally draws the knees up and over your shoulders and onto the ground, your head will have passed through the arch cantilevered for you by your forearms and the roll will be completed with you in a kneeling position. Congratulations. Familiarity through gentle repetition will soon allow you to remain tucked a little longer, causing the knees to remain in hover above the ground while the toes curl up thereby allowing the balls of the feet to be the landing contact. You may find that a little more impetus may ease things along as you add this ending to your roll, so think about

Rolls & Descents

extending the preparation: start from a crouch and gently sit, lay back and draw the knees up. Please, you are adding something new to the start, so only go as far as knees to chest at first. When you are confident with this as a continuous, flowing movement, and then start extending the ending.

When all this is working, perhaps try a standing start: from standing, bend the knees until you are crouching, and so on.

VERY IMPORTANT NOTE:-
At no stage did I write "go faster"!
Impetus and momentum will certainly help a complete move to reach its conclusion, but only if all the parts of that move are happening smoothly and flowing into each other and in the right order. So learn the parts and build up gradually. Any lumps or bumps in the constituent parts – or especially in the transitional moments from one part to the next – will get bigger and harder as you increase momentum.

Backward Shoulder Roll

Very similar to the backward roll, but this time both knees are drawn up and over *one* of your shoulders.

Lay on your back and decide which shoulder your knees are going to go over – for example, your right – and then incline your head to the other – in this example, you would try to place your left ear on your left shoulder. With the head safely out of the way to one (the left) side, start

Rolls & Descents

upping the draw on the knees to the chest, then shoulder, then ground to the other (right) side.

The arms are somewhat redundant as the head requires no gap for it to be made – the action of the roll over one shoulder allows the other shoulder to rise and so create head space. (Thus, for future reference, a way of regaining one's feet without having to lose one's rapier & dagger…)

To conclude the first part of this manual, and as just reward for being so patient, gentle reader, and practicing all the moves and techniques learnt thus far with an assiduousness and thoroughness such as to bring a tear to the eye of your patient tutor, I give you the move you have all been waiting for…

Unarmed 5 – Up & Down Slap

Unarmed 5 – Up & Down Slap

Slapping

A strike made with the palm or the back of the open hand.

The most abused bit of stage combat, the slap – seemingly innocuous – is potentially one of the most dangerous things to do to someone on stage. The reason for this is the amount of different injuries a slap can cause…

It's ridiculous. You suggest a poke in the eye or a kick in the balls and no-one says "Oh, don't worry about learning a tricky technique, just poke my eye/kick my balls." But with slapping, caution and common sense fly out of the window. A real slap is a real slap, it's real, and as such has no place in the make-believe, let's pretend world of acting where everything is illusion (truthful pretence, but pretence nonetheless).

If you see someone get slapped for real on stage – and you do know when it is real – you don't sit there thinking "that character deserved it" or "that character didn't deserve it" you sit there thinking "Ow! That must really have hurt that *actor*". Suddenly all suspension of disbelief has gone. The actors have failed. And they turn up in the next scene – *"the same, two years later"* – with four red stripes down their face.

And that is before we discuss injury. Put your right hand onto your left cheek. Start with the heel of the hand and

Unarmed 5 – Up & Down Slap

wiggle it around on your chin and jawbone. With it still in place, see what you can reach with your thumb. With little difficulty you can press your nose with a thumb knuckle and poke your eye with thumb tip. (You've probably realised by now where this is going.) Push the middle of your hand, the bit just before it becomes fingers, onto your cheekbone and discover how hard and painful those two bits coming into contact can be. With your fingers, find your ear, temple and eye. Finally, slip your hand down your face a little way and see how soon the little finger connects with the windpipe. (As you do that, note how the heel, and then the middle of your hand, brushes tantalisingly against your teeth and lips...)

It is possible to damage the cartilage of the larynx, break or dislocate the jaw, knock someone out by connecting with the point of the jaw, put a fracture into the cheekbone, blacken, scratch or remove the eye, drive teeth through lip/cheek, or remove some of them completely, and break the nose. And if you slightly cup your hand and clap it over someone's ear you can rupture their eardrum, rendering them partially or wholly deaf in that ear.

And all this without any training whatsoever.

Trust me; it is worth spending a little bit of time learning how to fake a slap.

Unarmed 5 – Up & Down Slap

The Up & Down Slap

Slapper stands opposite slappee, raises finger of left hand to line up slap, and cracks slappee across face with right hand.

The twenty-one word summary, above, conjures up a vivid picture in our mind. How many times have we seen the warning/threatening finger followed up by the action? And how many times have we seen the preparation of the action immediately prior to its conclusion? It is all perfectly natural – and that is why it works so well. Here is the film:

1. Close up – victims face pulled up to camera, the hand turning into threatening finger.
2. Cut to close up of aggressor's face – "*You dirty rat*"
3. Camera widens to take in aggressor raising hand – "*Why I oughtta...*"
4. Quick cut to victims face turning to horror
5. Quick cut to aggressor's hand flying out of shot – sound effect of slap
6. Cut to victim nursing side of face

We don't even have to see the impact; and in many cases the audience don't realise they *haven't* seen the impact…but it works.

So how do we do it on stage?

Unarmed 5 – Up & Down Slap

Exactly the same way: we set up the slap, give the audience enough time to think they are going to see a slap, then trick it so neatly that they believe they have.

Let's go back a bit. Given that we have the context and the scene, technically the first thing that happens is the raising of the threatening finger. But surely that is part of the scene? Yes, well it's both. The raised finger is a natural part of the scene but it also serves as a distance check.

Alternatively, we have a distance check that is disguised as a natural part of the scene...

For a moment let us take away the scene and the context and look solely at the technical:

Slapper is right-handed. Slapper stands with left foot forward. Slapper raises left hand to check distance with pointing forefinger and straight arm. Forefinger should be between 10–20 cm away from slappee's face.

With left foot forward, the left arm is 'longer' than the right, as the left shoulder is in front of the right shoulder. Without moving feet or body, if the right forefinger were extended it will only reach to the left wrist – another 20cm or so short of the victim's face. So any action with the right hand will be even safer than the threatening left forefinger – PROVIDING NOTHING IS DONE TO CLOSE THE DISTANCE.

Unarmed 5 – Up & Down Slap

So, the feet are set – left foot forward – the threatening left finger is extended, the distance is safe. The next thing to happen is the slapper's right hand is raised in a clear, pre-slap position over their right shoulder.

The slapping hand is then swung in a horizontal line in front of the slappee's face, which will be missed by 30–40cms. Providing nothing changes to alter the distance.

One or all of three things may happen:

- Slapper leans forward
- Slapper steps forward
- Slappee moves forward.

The first two are the most obvious worries, but the third option, though bizarre, is not unknown. The advice may be simply that once the distance has been set, do nothing – don't change a thing. I have found that telling someone to just do nothing doesn't work quite as well as giving them something active to do (positive negativity). In this case, to lean back as the action (the slap) happens. Quite natural for the slappee, but a very strange feeling for the slapper. So reinforce it: as you throw the slap, transfer all your weight to the back (right) foot. When you are first learning this technique, even go so far as to lift the left (front) foot off the floor by a few centimetres to get you used to leaning away.

Unarmed 5 – Up & Down Slap

So the distance has been checked, the slap is thrown, both parties are not moving in – sorry, actively moving away, how about the rest?

When slapping, as the hand contacts the face, its profile is altered by the movement of the face; as the face turns after impact, so the hand must follow that shape and the palm must turn to face the victim. From the victim's side, as the hand connects with the face, the head snaps round away from the side that has been struck – in this case, right hand slap to left cheek = head snaps to victim's right.

Step by step: - This is an example of a move that requires telegraphy – i.e. it depends on the audience being directed though the thought process:

1 - The hand
2 - The face
1 + 2 = There is *going to be* a slap...

The distance has been checked by the pointing finger of the non-slapping hand;

The slap is prepared with a big wind-up clearly showing the audience – and the victim – the open hand;

The slap is thrown, the victim reacts, and the slapping hand follows through, not pausing for a split second at the point of the cheat.

Unarmed 5 – Up & Down Slap

All we need now is the sound effect.

It is perfectly natural to swiftly place a hand on the body part that has just been stung, so the victim will use this normal movement to disguise the sound effect, or 'knap'. As the right hand is raised to the left, slapped, cheek, it glances off the open left hand. The resulting clap is a pretty accurate sound effect for a slap and, done at speed, is unnoticeable by the audience who, if it has been set up properly, are focussing on the area around the head where, they think, the contact is going to happen, not down by the hips where the clap is actually made. Obviously this clap cannot be prepped, as the audience will notice the penguin style flapping of the hands prior to clapping. In the same way, the head reaction cannot be prepped otherwise it will be obvious that it wasn't caused by the 'contact'.

This completes the first part of The Stage Combat Handbook.

Footwork 3 – Pass Steps & More

Part Two

The second part of The Stage Combat Handbook looks at extending the techniques and physical lexicon learned thus far.

There is a more *Gestalt* element to this section in that there is an assumption that the safety techniques are more ingrained at this stage. In other words, do not forget the safety lessons up to this point and always ensure that eye-contact, distance and communication are constantly implemented even if not explicitly referred to.

Footwork 3 – Pass Steps & More

Pass Step

To cover more distance – or to cover distance quickly - you can employ the 'pass step' to move forwards or backwards.

Moving forwards: this is led with back (non-sword) foot.

Start on guard, online. The non-sword foot passes in front of the sword foot and is placed, heel on the line, one hip width ahead of the sword foot.

You have made one pass step forward. You have the choice now of making another pass step forward – this time with the sword foot, to pass the non-sword foot – into on guard further forward, or you can take a pass step back(wards), with the non-sword foot, to recover into your original on guard.

Technical Distinction:

In modern fencing the two steps you have just learnt are classed as one pass-step in other words, a pass step is defined as two steps, the first crossing the legs and the second, moving in the same direction, uncrosses them. One pass step starts and finishes in on guard position; in stage combat the move is broken down so that you need to make two pass steps to resume an on guard.

Footwork 3 – Pass Steps & More

Should you feel the need to retreat more urgently, you may do so with pass steps: from on guard, pass the sword foot behind the non-sword foot, along your line, to complete one pass step back, and then complete a second pass step back, this time with the non-sword foot, to resume an on guard position.

As a cat moves, either walking or running, its head stays level, so that its eyes can remain steadily on its target, so the combatant moves along their line. You travel forwards and backwards as if between two sheets of glass, body width apart, and with a third sheet at head level, parallel to the ground, none of which must ever be broken by any lateral, side-to-side swaying, or vertical, up-and-down bobbing movement.

Abbreviations: the abbreviations used in this Handbook are mainly conventional, although some may be purely from the author's own personal choice. For the most part they are fairly obvious. It must, however, be noted that certain abbreviations have a higher frequency or tradition ranking – for example; on guard will always be assumed to mean the standard 'on guard online' of the fencer, therefore it is deemed superfluous to use OGOL, as OG will suffice. LFf/w (Left Foot Forward) would have to be added when applicable as the convention assumes all swordspeople to be right handed. Similarly, forward movement is assumed with a pass step, therefore the abbreviation PS is sufficient, while backwards movement

Footwork 3 – Pass Steps & More

takes the modification PSb/w. You are, of course, free to invent your own 'abbrev's' if you don't like mine!

(Thought: why is 'abbreviation' such a long word..?)

Footwork 3 – Pass Steps & More

Assuming you are **On Guard Online (OG)** with either **Right Foot Forward (OG)** or **Left Foot Forward (OGLFf/w)**:

Adv – (right foot, then left foot)
Adv – (right foot, then left foot)
PSb/w – (right foot)
PSb/w – (left foot)

This should have you finishing where you started.

Similarly:

PS
PS
Ret
Ret

Should bring you back to where you started.

For practice, do the above exercises both LFf/w and RFf/w, regardless of your own natural preference.

As a guide:

1 **PS** = 1 **Adv** *or* 1 **Ret**
1 **PS** = 1 foot movement
1 **Adv** *or* **Ret** = 2 foot movements.

Footwork 3 – Pass Steps & More

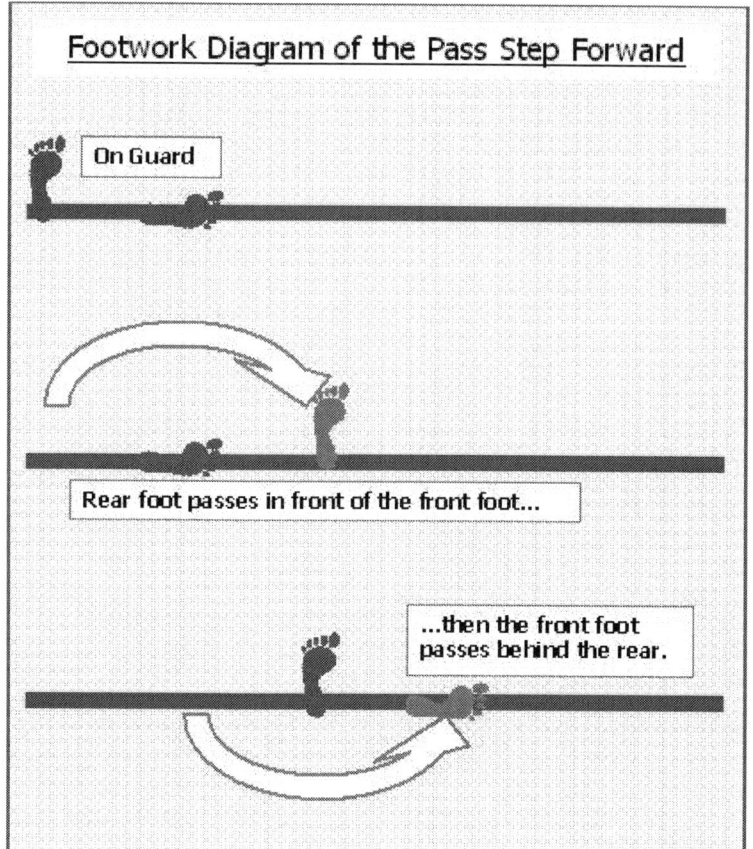

Diagram 8 – The Pass Step Forward

Lunge & Recover Forwards & Backwards

First a reminder – the last paragraph from Chapter iii in Part Two - '**Footwork 2 – Lunge & Recover**':-

> "Let us take time out to examine and define the term '**Recover**'.

Footwork 3 – Pass Steps & More

The definition is very strict and thus very simple: **_To return to On Guard._** So when you Lunge by stepping *forward* with the front foot, you recover by stepping *back* with the front foot."

By modifying the command 'Recover' (rec) to 'Recover Forward' (rec f/w) what happens? In this case, having lunged by moving the front foot forward, we recover forward by moving the *back* foot forward to regain On Guard further along the line.

Let's go back to the **Pass Step**.

1. **OG**
2. **PS**
3. **PS**

= Two steps forward to **On Guard**.

1. **OG**
2. **PS b/w**
3. **PS b/w**

= Two steps backwards to **On Guard**.

1. **OG**
2. **PS**
3. **Rec**

= One step forward & one step backwards to the original **On Guard**.

Footwork 3 – Pass Steps & More

1. **OG**
2. **PS b/w**
3. **Rec**

= One step backwards & one step forwards to the original **On Guard**.

Make sense?

*Back to the **Lunge**:*
1. **OG**
2. **Ext & lun**
3. **Rec**

= front foot **Lunge** followed by front foot return to original **On Guard**.

1. **OG**
2. **Ext & lun**
3. **Rec f/w**

= front foot **Lunge** followed by *back* foot moving up to a new **On Guard**.

Note – as we are in the section entitled 'Footwork 3', it must be noted that the term 'On Guard' here – while involving hands - primarily refers to foot positions. It is not at all unusual to recover forwards & backwards to different On Guard hand positions…

Re-read this section thus far before you read the next bit. I'll wait here. It is important that you are clear on the actions and the terms used to describe them before you move on.

Footwork 3 – Pass Steps & More

Pass Lunge
You can, of course, Pass Lunge. That is, having taken one pass step (either f/w or b/w); your front (lunging) foot is now behind your rear foot and so it must pass on its way to attaining lunge. From this lunge you will either rec or rec f/w directly to OG. In other words, you do not recover to a cross legged position and then pass step to get to an OG.

Then there is the Step Lunge.
Ext(end) & lun(ge) in the approved fashion; now bring the rear foot up to the rec f/w position while at the same time raising the non-sword arm to its usual OG position, *but maintain the extension with the sword arm*; now simply lunge again with the front foot, dropping the n/s arm. This can be perpetuated indefinitely until you finally succeed in running your opponent through, or disappear into the wings.

And lastly in this section…

Reverse Lunge
Any ideas?

Yep. Ext as usual, but now the lunge is done by shooting back the rear leg to drop down into the lunge. A stop-hit move to impale your opponent as they try, for example, to slice your head off. I.e. it depends on them walking (or lunging) onto your point (while you, having drawn this attack from them, avoid it by ducking).

Footwork 3 – Pass Steps & More

Question: Is this move offensive or defensive?

Clue: think about the term 'simultaneous counter-attack'.

Answer: Both. It is defensive if you are reacting to their attack, but it is offensive if you deliberately drew that attack out of them with the intention to duck & kill.

More to re-read and ponder.

Back to the point.

You have extended and reverse lunged; next instruction is 'Recover'. What do you do?

Congratulations if your answer was moving the rear foot back to the original OG. (If you are not convinced just go back and read again the definition at the top of this piece.)

It may very well be that your devious trickery has failed and your reverse lunge has been foiled; therefore, to recover *(forwards)* would be suicide, bringing you up close and personal with your assailant. At this point you would choose to recover b/w. And of course in this case moving the front foot back has to be stated in the instruction for clarification purposes…

Re-read and make sure you know and understand this stuff before you move on.

Footwork 4 – Other On Guards

On Guard Neutral

In the Basic section we looked at a basic all-purpose on guard foot position. Truth to tell, this is the hardest of the on guards we will be looking at. It should, paradoxically, be learnt first as by the time you move on to weapons and systems which require the following simpler variations, these new on guard foot positions should fall into place relatively quickly and not distract from the simultaneous learning of parries and strokes.

In the all-purpose on guard the heel of the back foot and the length of the front foot stood on an imaginary tightrope on which stood in front of you, your opponent.

Such guards are referred to as 'online'. The feet occupy a single line of attack, directed straight towards your opponent. Excellent for times when handling a single weapon whilst dealing with a single opponent…

Online guard positions have the advantage over other positions when facing a single assailant and you are armed with one weapon in that it keeps that weapon between you and your attacker whilst presenting the minimum amount of target area. Excellent for fast and sudden linear movement forwards & backwards and corresponding stability, however, you are vulnerable and limited in sideways movement, particularly if you wish to sustain the

Footwork 4 – Other On Guards

online relationship with your partner. And you are potentially very unstable laterally.

In circumstances when the weapon requires both hands, (Quarterstaff, Baseball bat, pool cue, etc.), or when two or more opponents are coming at you from different angles (different lines of attack), or if the weapon is less than standard (Bike chain, frying pan, broken bottles), or in fact, any number of reasons where coming on guard online is not the most effective stance to adopt.

On guard neutral utilises a tightrope at right angles to your on guard online position: stand facing a single partner square on. Now simply step one foot out to one side so that your heels are slightly more than shoulder width apart. Flex the knees until the kneecaps are directly over your toes and ensure that your weight is equally distributed over both legs and along each foot (50/50 left & right; 50/50 heel & toe).

On guard neutral describes itself beautifully – a stance of readiness, giving little away as to intention or direction while at the same time preparing you to move in any direction to attack, defend or avoid. Its two inherent weaknesses are

1. You are unstable forwards/backwards and liable to moments of being off-balance – one of those directions being directly towards a (possibly armed) opponent;

Footwork 4 – Other On Guards

2. You present maximum target area.

On Guard Offline

In compass terms, we have on guard positions in which the feet occupy either the North-South line (on guard online) or the East-West line (on guard neutral).

Neither is perfect – they each have advantages and disadvantages, strengths and weaknesses, times when they will save you and times when they won't help quite as much.

On advantage with coming on guard online when armed with single sword is that it maintains the point and edge of the weapon at a station closer to your partner then the target area, i.e....you.

What if armed with sword and dagger? Coming on guard online would put your sword between you and your attacker but you may as well leave the dagger sheathed as it takes up post behind you...

And while coming on guard neutral will certainly put the dagger into play in front of your body, the open stance means that your target area is exposed, and the discrepancy in length of the sword and the dagger means that you are attempting to operate two fighting distances at the same time – when the dagger is useful you will be too close to use the sword comfortably and at sword distance the dagger is redundant.

Footwork 4 – Other On Guards

So we use on guard offline.

Stand with your feet East-West (on guard neutral). You have a sword in your sword hand and a dagger in what will henceforth be referred to as your 'dagger hand'. *('dagger hand' is obviously the hand which holds the dagger. In this instance, Sword & Dagger, the tacit inference is that the dagger is the secondary weapon and as such is relegated to the weaker hand. If the arming was 'single dagger', the stronger hand would usually be the 'dagger hand' – note that the 'dagger hand' can change during a fight, for example if the sword is lost and the dagger is then moved to what was the sword hand.)* Now step backward with your sword leg. Heels still slightly wider than hip width, weight still evenly distributed, knees still going out over the toes. There are two ways of looking at this foot position: 1. you are either standing on your compass with your feet occupying the North-East/South-West line (or the North-West/South-East line); 2. That instead of being on a single tightrope with your opponent, you are now on two tightropes - or rail tracks – which you are sharing with your opponent.

At this stage it is easier to work in the latter mode and imagine a single set of rail tracks which you and your partner are sanding on, facing each other, each with their sword foot set behind them and their dagger foot in front.

In this foot position bring sword and the dagger up in front of you by straightening your arms to the extend

Footwork 4 – Other On Guards

position. Aim both of your points at your partners' navel. You have your arms parallel at shoulder height, your hands at shoulder width apart, the points angled slightly in and down towards the target. If you, from this position, slowly start to flex the elbows outwards and allow the hands to lower and the points to stay on target you will find a stance at which the two points are about level – i.e. the same distance away from you. You have to keep the arms parallel to the ground and not allow the elbows to either point towards the ground or come any closer to your body. You will feel a little like you are resting the underside of your arms on a level bar counter.

If you attempt to get into this hand position by raising the sword and dagger from a dangling downwards position, the tendency is to move like a cowboy quick-draw artist – you keep the elbows tucked in to your body and the point invariably will aim up, usually at your partner's face. Both of these are to be avoided.

Important things to notice about getting into this on guard position:

1. Start in on guard neutral and move the *sword foot back*.
2. Extend sword and dagger, arms parallel to ground and to each other – the hands stay at shoulder width apart.
3. Ensure points are aiming *down*, at partner's navel.

Footwork 4 – Other On Guards

4. Slide your elbows out (along the bar counter) until sword and dagger points are about level.

Without weapons you would look a little like you are astride a horse with a large beach ball in your arms.

Ultimately you will be able to assume this position automatically once you have built in the physical memory to your body, but please include the feature of stepping *backwards* into position with the sword foot and resist the urge to learn this by stepping *forwards* with the dagger foot.

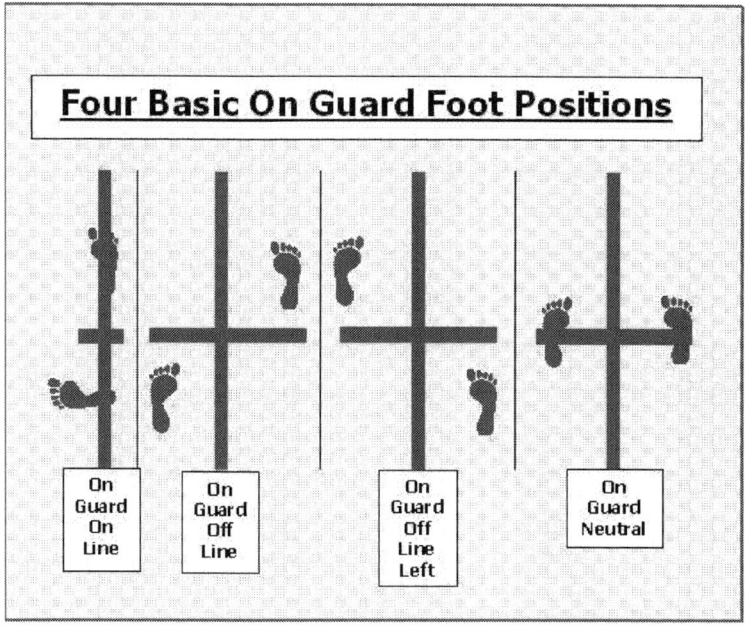

Diagram 9 – Four On Guard Foot Positions

Unarmed 6 - Taking a Knap

The Importance of Sound Effects

Some years ago the vice-principal of a leading London Drama Academy asked me to set a tiny piece of action for a final year play he was directing. On my arrival I was delighted to find that the two fighters were top stage combatants. The scene – A has B at gunpoint;

1. B places jewels on chair at A's request;
2. A goes to pick them up, glances down and
3. B punches A's head.

Simplicity itself…

We were left to it and had it set and rehearsed in due course. The director was called, witnessed our effort and pronounced that it needed to be and I quote:
"more…err…vicious…shocking…err…well…*more.*"

I took the note and leapt onto the stage to join the two confused and crestfallen actors – after all, they felt that they had executed the moment superbly.

My instruction to B was this: "When you hit him, shout. Doesn't matter what you shout, just make a loud noise."

They did it again, exactly as before, except that this time, as B delivered the punch, he shouted loudly. The director leapt from his seat yelling "YES! Brilliant – that's *it!*" shook everybody's hand and went for coffee.

Unarmed 6 - Taking a Knap

The moral – sound effects sell fights. The ears are very powerful receptors and require appropriate stimulus for the fight to work to its best effect. Put your favourite fight scene on and mute the sound...the grittiest fight suddenly becomes meaningless and, usually, comedic.

And it doesn't matter so much that the sound effect is totally accurate, more that there is a sound effect there. (There is, after all, only one thing that sounds like nasal bone being splintered under knuckles and that is nasal bone being etc...)

Lacking the luxury afforded on film and television of an editing suite, dubbing engineers and soundtrack, actors on stage have to create the sound effects as they go along.

As we go through various techniques I will attempt to include notes on sound effects where appropriate, but let me set this particular scene by first covering some basics.

Knap - Definitions
Definition: - A 'knap' is the simulated sound of an impact.

Rules:-

1. There must be a sound effect to complete the illusion;
2. It is more important that there *is* a sound effect then that the sound effect is 100% accurate;

Unarmed 6 - Taking a Knap

3. Do not repeat - done proficiently any knap can escape the audience's perception; done brilliantly, a knap repeated once may avoid detection on its repeat; done a third time, however, no matter how well it is executed, the knap will be seen.

Basic varieties are as follows:

First Party Knap – the attacker makes the sound.
Second Party Knap – the recipient makes the sound.
Joint Knap – the attacker and the victim combine to make the sound.

The notation convention is:
1PK = First Party Knap,
2PK = Second Party Knap
1&2PK = Joint Knap.

It is of course possible for third, fourth, fifth etc. PK's but the more people involved in trying to create the illusion the more chances there are of it going wrong.

Types of knap

Claphand Knap – the sound effect is generated by one person clapping their hands together. Usually the victim as a **2PK** to a head punch or a slap to the face, but can be done as a **1PK** to a face kick etc.

Sliphand Knap – specialised **1PK** Claphand (see below)

Unarmed 6 - Taking a Knap

Body Knap – any knap in which the effect is generated by striking a part of a body with a hand

FX Knap – any knap utilising mechanical aid

Contact Knap – describes a knap which is self-generated by a contact move

Secret Knap – the *botta segretta* of the Fight Director – any knap which is impossible because all hands have weapons in or are in plain view etc.

Botta Segretta: Italian, trans. 'secret move'. In the old days, fight masters would put about rumours that they had a secret, unbeatable move, which they would only teach students who proved their loyalty by staying with the master, paying them all the while.

Which Knaps Work When, Why & How
"The audience must never know." Obvious, really…

So, how does it "not show from the front"?

There are only a few very simple concepts to understand:

Masking – the knap is hidden from the audience's view by something or someone;

Blocking – the choreography, calls for someone to move into, or transit through, a position which masks the knap;

Unarmed 6 - Taking a Knap

Distraction – the audience's attention is subtly and deliberately directed to a specific area while the cheat happens in a different space;

Telegraphing – some moves work best because you have signalled the audience about what to expect – as a result, they have completed the move in their mind before it has been done – effectively you have made them blink and they have missed it. Alternatively, some moves work best when they are not expected at all, the audience are left amazed at something that has just happened out of the blue and, as a result, can't look for the cheat because it is already history;

Technique – the timing, speed, slickness, dexterity, skill and art which can only come from hours of patient rehearsal is, ultimately, the only element which can guarantee a satisfactory performance. Inextricably tied to technique is…

Disguise – the knap must happen as part of the natural shape of the movements the audience are watching. Hands swinging out from the victim's sides to prep the knap will alert the spectator/viewer. As will a claphand knap, for example, with no follow through – by which I mean a person having their face slapped will probably raise one or both hands to the side of the face which has just been struck. A natural and wholly instinctive reaction which the audience will expect to see. And if, in the midst of that

Unarmed 6 - Taking a Knap

action, one hand happens to fleetingly glance off the other and make a sound, the audience will have no choice but to believe that the sound actually came from the slap, because there was nothing out of the ordinary - nothing unusual - about the reaction. If the person getting slapped had only clapped their hands together and not followed through with a 'real' reaction, the audience will register an arm/shoulder movement which had no connection to the process of being slapped and they will, therefore, spot the cheat.

Practice knaps by yourself. They nearly always require some sleight of hand. A discreet claphand flowing into a slap reaction; a chest knap as you jab or kick air. The more you practice the less you will need to think about it when it is called for.

But please, make sure that no-one is looking…

FOOTWORK 5 – THE STAR & COMPASS

Avoidances

We have already examined one method of foiling an attack – by blocking or parrying it.

There is another way of not getting hit and that is simply by not being in the target space when the attack arrives. These techniques are called **Avoidances.**

It may at first seem strange that this subject appears as a sub-heading of 'Footwork' – I aim to clarify this first.

The characteristic of any attack from any weapon falls into three categories:

1. Impact – a fist, quarterstaff or sword pommel, for example;
2. Penetration – finger poke to the eye, thrust from a sword, or a bullet, for example;
3. Laceration – fingernails down the face, a cut from a sword or a lash from a whip, for example;

Some weapons may have more than one characteristic or even primary and secondary characteristics, however, they all rely one thing – the line of attack. This is the line drawn from the point of launch to the point of contact, usually either straight or circular (the difference between a thrust and a cut with a sword, or a hook and a jab with a fist) while we usually think of a small and specific target area

Footwork 5 – The Star & Compass

some weapons have an expanding target zone – for example, shotgun pellets spreading as soon as the leave the muzzle, shock-waves, sound, debris and shrapnel following the detonation of a grenade or bomb.

It is important to recognise the line of the attack in order to most effectively block it. And also how to avoid it.

We have all seen movies in which bullets are avoided by twisting the body and watching them pass by in slo-mo. Or where the boxer evades punches to their face by moving their head sideways or backwards.

In reality, once the bullet has left the barrel, no human can react quickly enough to get out of its way; and when a boxer learns to 'bob and weave' or 'duck and dive' it will be backed up with a blocking arm and/or some avoiding footwork.

In swordplay, the attacks will be either lateral or vertical – a thrust is a lateral attack moving in & out; cuts which are avoided rather than parried are differentiated by being referred to as 'slashes'. The slash may be lateral left to right or right to left, or vertical, high to low or low to high. Targets for slashes, as a guide:

- Head – may be slashed side to side and ducked
- Head – may be slashed vertically and avoided to the side

Footwork 5 – The Star & Compass

- Waistline (stomach/side/back) – target may be displaced backwards – away from the attacker
- Feet – the classic jump over the blade!

Slashes can also be made diagonally, downwards, say high right to low left (HiR-LoL), or upwards, say low right to high left (LoR-HiL). These slashes are usually set in the choreography to ensure that the blade is moving away from the defender (as well as the defender moving away from the blade).

Important note: It is surprisingly easy to hit a moving target! It is imperative that the slash is prepped in line with the target and the attackers eyes remain fixed at the space where the target was – rather like seeing an after-image of an actor when their spotlight is snapped off. Do not follow the defender/target with your eyes as they avoid – where your eyes lead, your blade will surely follow…

Ducking

Asked what they think a duck is in order to avoid a swinging, haymaker type punch to the head, the majority of students bend from the waist to drop their head out of the target area. The major concern here is that the eyes are inevitably directed away from the action (usually to the floor) with the result that the defender cannot tell:

1. If they have ducked low enough to effectively avoid the attack;

Footwork 5 – The Star & Compass

2. If it is safe to move their head back into the target area.

I have encountered problems with both of these issues and have found that the best way of teaching the duck is as a piece of footwork: either flex both knees, keeping the body square-on to where it is facing, or twist from the feet through 90°, flex both legs and place the rear knee on the floor. **But in both instances I stress that one hand must be placed on the floor.** This not only guarantees that the head has travelled far enough to be safely out of the target zone, but it also aids balance and a safer recovery. And with legs doing the work the head is free to look at the attacker and see when it is safe to come out of the duck. (For a more in-depth look at this technique see the relevant section *Ducking a Punch* in the chapter *Unarmed 9 – Blocked Punches 2*.)

Lateral Avoidances

While ducking involves the displacement of the target area in a downwards direction, it is also possible to execute avoidances to the side.

There are three directions to either side available to effect an avoidance – to the side & forwards, to the side and backwards & directly out to the side; there are also three different paths to move in each of these directions, depending on preference, efficacy and choreography – Lunging, Slipping & Crossing.

Footwork 5 – The Star & Compass

To simplify the explanation of each possible variation it is perhaps easiest to introduce at this stage a powerful teaching and annotating tool – the Star.

In the introduction to this Handbook, when we looked at positions on the stage, we defined the Actor's Compass. It is a simple and very effective tool for describing and annotating an actor's position and movements on stage. It hinges on having a fixed point – the audience – from which to orient the positions.

The Star is basically the Fighter's Compass – a version of the Actor's Compass.

The eight cardinal points are:

- Front (F)
- Front Right (FR)
- Right (R)
- Back Right (BR)
- Back (B)
- Back Left (BL
- Left (L)
- Front Left (FL)

Footwork 5 – The Star & Compass

The Fighter's Compass

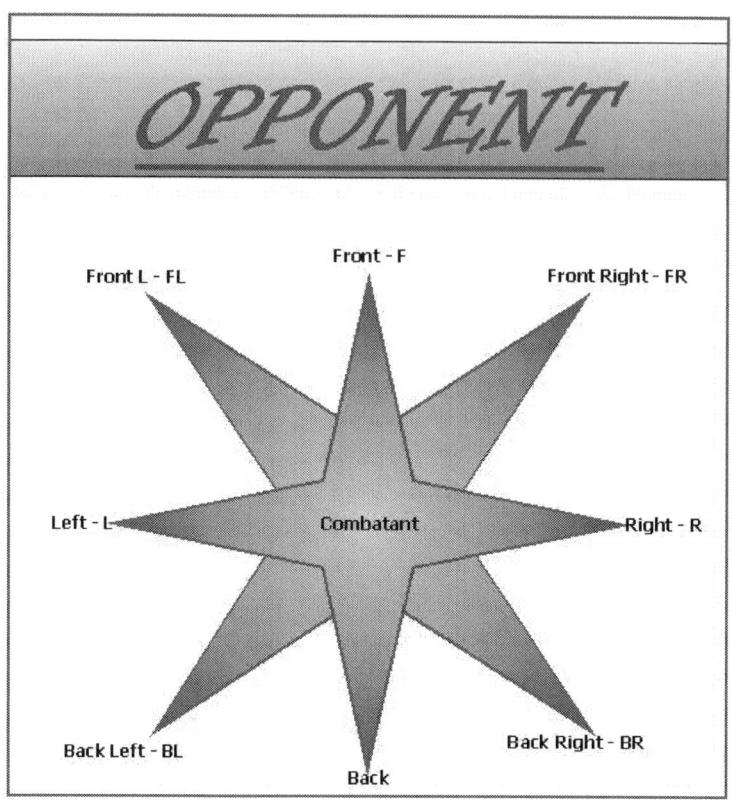

Diagram 10 – The Fighter's Compass

Footwork 5 – The Star & Compass

Star Footwork

The star shape has a long and distinguished career in sports as a template for footwork practice and its application to stage combat choreography and training is only fitting and natural.

It is used by many practitioners and has been defined in several ways: what follows is the author's interpretation and usage.

Quite simply, the star defines eight destinations (the star's points) for the working foot. The supporting foot will pivot and adjust accordingly to the movement of the working foot. The big question is what do use as 'front'? The Actor's Compass uses the audience – naturally so, as every move and position an actor takes onstage must take into account the audience (even if the choice is to exclude them). As the majority of fights involve two protagonists, some practitioners use the opponent's position as 'front'. This orientation point then becomes a variable, but as the focus in a fight is on the opponent, a constant variable. Both of these options work, however, they share the same drawback: frequently, and at various times, neither of these 'fronts' actually correspond to the direction the fighter is actually *facing*. The author's favoured implementation, therefore, is to work with a variable 'front' position based on the actual 'front' as faced by the individual after each completed piece of footwork *which involves pivoting*.

Footwork 5 – The Star & Compass

So if the fight starts (usually) with both fighters coming on guard facing each other, then 'front' is where the other person is standing until there is a 'pivot' – a change of alignment, which may involve one or both fighters.

Two new terms are added to one familiar friend:

1. **Lunge**: moving the working foot away from the supporting foot;
2. **Slip**: moving the working foot behind the supporting foot;
3. **Cross**: moving the working foot in front of the supporting foot.

This applies to any on guard position and also to any foot position. Please bear with the convention that assumes all fighters to be right handed and footed. And also remember that the on guard position can make a difference.

- To avoid to, or attack from the right you would Lunge Right or LunR.
- To avoid to, or attack from the left you would Lunge Left or LunL.
- If you were on guard online (with single sword, for example) a standard lunge would become a Lunge Front or LunF.
- If left-handed and on guard online, a standard lunge would still be Lunge Front or LunF.

Footwork 5 – The Star & Compass

- On guard neutral and attacking with a sword in the right hand it would be Lunge Front or LunF for a standard lunge.
- On guard neutral and attacking with a sword in the left hand it would be Lunge Front or LunF for a standard lunge.
- The Star Footwork System covers all footwork – offensive or defensive – from any position.
- Some moves will require pivoting on the supporting foot for comfort and health reasons.

Remember, the Star moves with you and its centre remains directly underneath you while 'front' can change.

The choreology look confusing at first sight, however, bear in mind, from any start position either foot can travel away from, behind or in front of the other, and the star annotation system can track it. Incredible!

Also note that the supporting foot must always be allowed to pivot when necessary for comfort and safety.

Fight notation or Choreology: the assumption is that the combatant(s) is/are right-footed (for no better reason than that the majority are). Therefore the footwork is notated and taught from that point of view and any ambiguity is resolved by stating 'left foot' if required. LunF (lunge front will normally be with the right foot; if we intend it to be executed with the left we must say so – LflunF. Of course, if you are left-footed, please feel free to reverse this convention for your own personal use.

Footwork 5 – The Star & Compass

List of common star foot movements is as follows:

lunF – lunge front
lunFR – lunge front right
lunR – lunge right
lunBR – lunge back right
lunB – lunge back
LFlunB – left foot lunge back
lunBL – lunge back left
lunL – lunge left
lunFL – lunge front left
LFlunF – left foot lung front

XFR – cross front right – left foot passes in front of the right to the FR position
XFL – cross front left – right foot passes in front of the left to the front left position
XR – cross right – left foot passes in front of the right to the R position
XL – cross left – right foot passes in front of the left to the L position
XBR – cross back right – left foot passes in front of the right to the BR position
XBL – cross back left – right foot passes in front of the left to the BL position
XB – cross back – right foot passes in front of the left to the B position
LFXB – left foot cross back left – left foot passes in front of the right to the B position

Footwork 5 – The Star & Compass

It is more unusual – but not unheard of – to travel the following paths:

RFXBR – right foot cross back right – right foot passes in front of the left to the BR position

LFXBL – left foot cross back left – left foot passes in front of the right to the BL position

RFXR – right foot cross right – right foot passes in front of the left to the R position

LFXL – left foot cross left – left foot passes in front of the right to the L position

And even…

RFXFR/RFXF – right foot cross front right/front – full 360° pivot anticlockwise

LFXFL/LFXF – left foot cross front left/front – ditto clockwise.

SlipBR – slip back right – left foot passes behind the right to the BR position

SlipBL – slip back left – right foot passes behind the left to the BL position

SlipR – slip right – left foot passes behind the right to the R position

SlipL – slip left – right foot passes behind the left to the L position

SlipFR – slip front right - left foot passes behind the right to the FR position

SlipFL – slip front left – right foot passes behind the left to the FL position

Footwork 5 – The Star & Compass

SlipF – slip front – right foot passes behind the left to the F position

LFSlipF – left foot slip front – left foot passes behind the right to the F Position

Note: the bringing of one foot to the other so that both feet are together is called *rassemblement*, (abbr. *Rass*) and appears in notation as RtoLRass – Right (foot) to Left (foot) rassemblement or LtoRRass.

A quick recap:
There are two or three schools of thought as to how the star should be oriented: there are some as say that, like the actor's compass, Front should correspond to DS – where the audience is. Of course, there is a potential flaw here when working in-the-round…
Some say that Front should correspond to where the attacker is, however, potential problems here with multiple assailants or when continuing movement in another direction i.e. running away (flee avoidance).
My personal preference is that Front is wherever you are facing at the start of the choreography and changes following any pivot.
So the 'flee' avoidance would be written:

1. XB (right foot passes in front of the left to get to the Back position)
2. Piv180 (turn your back to opponent – new Front position)
3. Rpt PSs (repeat pass steps forward away from attacker).

Footwork 5 – The Star & Compass

Or:
1. Piv180 (turning the body first, pivoting on the feet and finding a new Front)
2. Rpt PSs (run away)

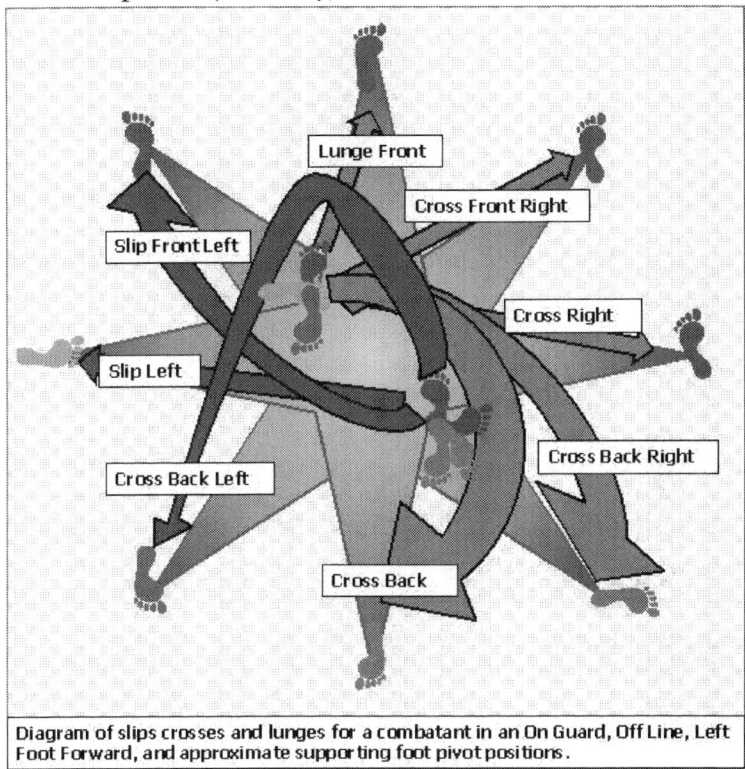

Diagram of slips crosses and lunges for a combatant in an On Guard, Off Line, Left Foot Forward, and approximate supporting foot pivot positions.

Diagram 11 – Slips, Crosses and a Lunge

Footwork 5 – The Star & Compass

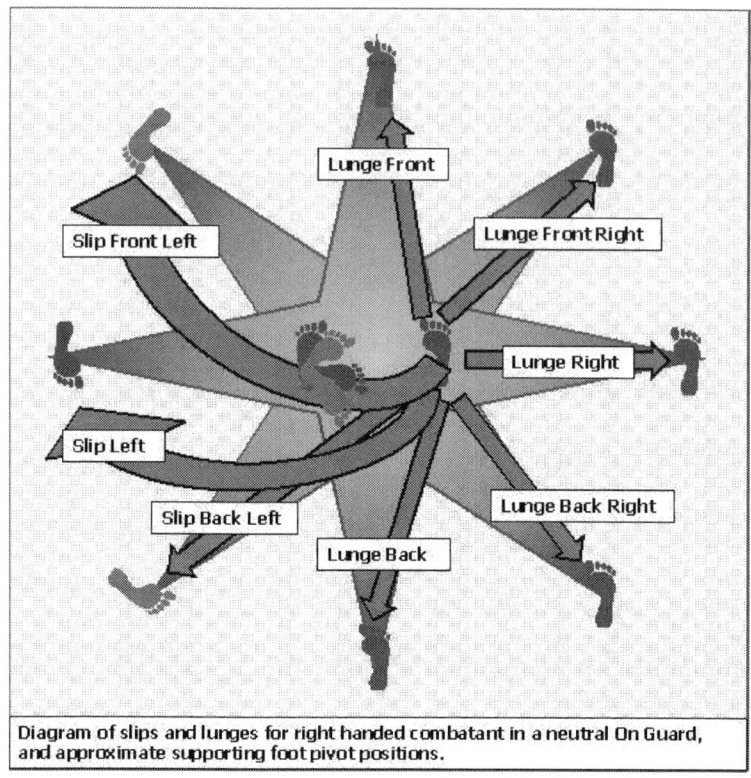

Diagram 12 – Lunges and Slips

Fingerwork 4 – Disengage & Coupé

Engage

To engage, in swordy terms, merely means for the opposing blades to be in contact. Two combatants may come on guard opposite each other and warily stalk without actual contact; or they may choose to touch the other's blade perhaps to try to control it or to provoke a reaction.

In this example we shall assume that two right-handed fighters are facing off and that A contacts – engages – B's blade and uses their sword to move B's blade so that it point off-target past A's sword-side. In other words, A engages in 3.

If B were to extend and lunge in this position, their sword would simply pass A quite harmlessly as A, engaged in 3, has effectively parried B's attack before it has been launched.

To become threatening and effective, B must manoeuvre their blade so that it is no longer 'parried' and can come online for a hit.

Disengage

One trick to achieve this is called the disengage:

A & B's blades are engaged – that is, they are touching. A's sword is basically in a Parry 3 position (on their sword-side, point up and pommel down) while B is ineffective

Fingerwork 4 – Disengage & Coupé

with their point resting against A's forté, aimed at thin air off to A's sword-side.

What B does is this: using the sword fingers to loosen their grip on the sword, they allow the point of their weapon to drop below the opposition pommel and then bring it up again to the inside of the forté and in a threatening position, leaving A's blade harmlessly – and uselessly – out to their sword-side. This is the 'disengage', or degagé, – a tiny, circular movement described by the point of the sword which (in the high line) makes a tiny circle from one side of the opposing blade, just under the pommel to the other side. From being controlled, B is back in control!

The disengage can be used in all four lines, high & low, inside & outside:

The movement of the point is as tiny as it can be – barely enough to clear the pommel. As we have covered, to escape from 3 the point moves in an anticlockwise circle under the pommel; from 4 the point describes a tiny clockwise circle under the pommel; from 1 the circle is anticlockwise over the pommel and from 2, clockwise over the pommel.

Coupé

There is an alternative to the disengage when engaged in either of the high lines and that is the 'coupé', or cutover. When engaged – or parried – you will feel the firmness or pressure of your partner's blade. Using this pressure, slide your blade up your partner's until it just comes over the tip, from there, bring the blade down as close to the inside of your partner's blade as possible. *Do not go to any other line*

Fingerwork 4 – Disengage & Coupé

than the one from which you started. So, engaged in three, coupé and come on target in three, or engaged in four, coupé and come on target in four.

A coupé from engagement in three and coming online to four, or vice versa, is extremely dangerous as it runs a high risk of taking the point of the sword across the line of the face.

UNARMED 7 - CAT FIGHTING

Foot Stamp – Up & Down
In an up & down configuration with the stamper DS, following eye-contact, spot a mark on the floor DS of victim's foot and stamp sharply *allowing the foot to bounce off the stage and into the air*. Reaction: sharply pull foot off the ground, vocalise and refer (i.e. point to it or grab it). The stampee is lifting their foot off the floor in their reaction therefore the stamper cannot leave their stamping foot on the ground is it then should have 'trapped' the stampee's foot, making it impossible to move. This is a tiny detail which is often overlooked – very often by the audience; however, it will have jarred slightly in their minds and lead to a lack of belief in the move and therefore the entire scene.

Foot Stamp – Profile
In profile: again, following eye-contact look for a mark on the floor immediately DS of the target. Aiming at the US foot and stamping the space between the two can be very forgiving as the victim's DS foot will add masking to the disguise of the move. As above, ensure that actions and reactions are consistent and 'real'.

Foot Stamp – ITR
Actually, done well either of the preceding techniques will work in-the-round, depending as they obviously do on the speed of the move leaving the audience behind and

therefore missing the instant of the 'impact'. This variation is a slower, sadistic version which specifically traps the victim's foot. It requires care and precision and is taught thus. Aggressor stands with the toes of the stamping foot against the toes of the foot to be stamped, both feet in line. The physical contact allows the stamper to know the precise location of the target without a visual check. The initial stamp is exactly the same as the 'Ad' move in 'Advance': the heel of the stamping foot replaces the ball of the foot which now will be hovering above the toes of the victim's. Quickly and gently lay the sole onto the victim's foot without putting any weight on it. In this case, the point is that the stamper is holding the foot down and applying progressive pain so the reactions can be with anything other than the actual foot, probably with references.

Bite – Your Lips
Version 1 of the bite effect has the biter taking hold of the target flesh (arm/leg/etc.), baring their teeth and closing their mouth on the target. As the closing takes place, so the biter pushes their lips forward to come between them and the target and in fact a vicious gumming or sucking occurs. In this – and all other versions of the bite – the pain is referenced by the victim who can react with any part of their body other than the bit being bitten. Take care – it is easy to accidentally pull the target away from the mouth and the subsequent reattachment can be genuinely painful and bruising, mainly for the biter.

Bite – Your Thumb

This variation has the biter again gripping the target area, but, hidden from the audience, lays their thumb along the target area and after baring their teeth, sinks them into their own digit.

Bite – Ever Widening

This version of the bite follows the same beginnings…grab target area, bare teeth and now lay the target into your mouth with the teeth still bared, lips drawn back. And continue to force your mouth open while holding the target flesh in place.

These variations suit different situations and different individuals – choose wisely!

Eye Poke - Up & Down

With the poker DS of the pokee: poker raises hand in 'victory salute' in line with the victim's face but well out of distance. Without moving the hand towards the face, simply dip the two outstretched finger from the vertical to the horizontal and back to vertical. This is a telegraphed move with the prep deliberate and the cheat happening quickly.

With the poker US of the pokee: ensure that the prep can be seen by the audience over the victim's head and the dip drops the fingers below the head from the audience's point of view.

Unarmed 7 - Cat Fighting

These are double eye pokes, in that two eyes are getting poked at the same time.

Eye Poke – Profile

This is a single poke to the eye although it generally works better using two fingers. Poker raises US hand with fore and middle finger extended and together, like two-thirds of a Boy Scout salute. Ensure that the prep can be seen, again, we are telegraphing this move. The two fingers are then poked into air on the US side of the victim's head. Speed is not essential here, however, accuracy is.

The actual target is at a point where a line from the top of the victim's ear and travelling US parallel to the ground bisects a line travelling vertically from the outside edge of the victim's shoulder.

Alternatively, we can engage Polly once again to sit on the victim's shoulder, not quite as tall as the victim's head, and poke her on the beak!

Safety: check the Sequence of Events - Eye-contact; prep; the attacker now moves their eyes to the actual target area; the poke; rec/react.

Scratch to Side of Face

Aggressor makes a claw of their working hand and closes in on the side of the victim's face. As they do so, they curl the fingertips over so that it is the first knuckles which contact the side of the head just above the hairline (or where the hairline was…). Victim lays palm of their hand over the aggressor's – usually the hand on the same side of the body as the attacked cheek, but sometimes the opposite works better. The victim can also place the palm of the other hand over the back of the first to add emphasis or dramatic purpose. As in the testicle grab in the RofE section, aggressor now uncurls the fingers to flatten the hand as they pull their hand downwards while pushing against the victim's hand, directing the energy away from the face and down. This must be a swift action and while there may be a sliding knap from the hand contact, the victim must emit an audible, sucking in of the breath knap to add to the illusion. This drawing of the breath in between the teeth should be accompanied with a head reaction that moves swiftly upwards and in the opposite direction of the scratch. Once safely disconnected from each other's hand contact, the aggressor should resume the claw shape and show it while the victim's hands should flatten against their cheek.

Note: while the real reaction may be to go with the direction of the scratch, theatrically it works far better in opposition; and the quick sucking in of breath over the teeth is the perfect knap.

Scratch to Front of Face

As above, the attacker demonstrates 'the claw' and closes in on the target. Curling the fingertips, they place the first knuckles on the victim's forehead; the victim, overlapping

Unarmed 7 - Cat Fighting

their hands, covers the attacking hand; aggressor straightens their fingers, pushes back into the victim's hand and pulls sharply down – pushing into the hands and away from the face. Again, the reaction must be vocalised with a sharp sucking in of the breath (the higher pitched the better!), the claw shape resumed as soon as the hand is clear of the face, and the victim's hands flatten onto the 'scratched' surface.

Fingerwork 5 – Counter Parries

Fingerwork 5 – Counter Parries

Counter-parry

The counter-parry is also referred to as the circular parry. This differentiates it from the parries learnt thus far which are called 'lateral parries'. (*Lateral vs. Circular: there is sometimes confusion here because the path to the lateral parry may involve a bit of a circular motion – going from P3 to P2, for example, the path is semi-circular. Please accept that for a parry to qualify as circular, the blade must complete a full, 360° rotation.*)

The counter-parry takes the blade from one parry position, through a complete 360° rotation and finishes in the same parry position. (You will need to put a little wrist flick somewhere in the rotation to allow you to complete the action without either dislocating your wrist, or letting the point drift into a dangerous position.)

Here is where the swordy fun really begins: imagine that you have drawn swords with an opponent; you have raised your blade and engaged them in 3 so that your right, pronated hand has, with the cutting edge of your blade, led their sword off of your body to the green zone beyond your sword side high line.

They now execute a disengage – circling the point of their weapon under the pommel of yours – and while you now stand in a perfect P3 position. Their blade is aimed at your sword-side chest.

Fingerwork 5 – Counter Parries

What do you do?

Two choices, really. Either you move your P3 laterally to P4, taking their point all the across your red zone body until you reach the green outside your non-sword side. Or you whirl your blade in a shamelessly theatrical – but very effective 360° circle – to recapture their blade and push it to safety in back in 3!

These grandiose, circular moves – spinning the sword from a parry position through 360°, the point travelling in a huge circle, back to the original parry position – are known as 'counter parries'. Or 'circular parries'.

Counter-parry Practice

With sword in hand, go to parry three (P3). Now move towards a wall until you are standing in front of it, square on, with your knuckle-guard a couple of centimetres away from it. Slowly and carefully push the blade away and down; just before it points to the floor, twist the wrist, and then carry on with the circle, bringing the blade up in front of your body and back to three.

Repeat this exercise with parries 1, 2, and 4.

Then try with 6, 7, & 8.

Do not try with 5 & 5a...

Fingerwork 5 – Counter Parries

The exercise to perfect the technique is simple: assume a parry – say P3; stand in front of a wall; move towards the wall until you are nearly touching it; now impel the blade to move to the outside by the tip while keeping your sword-hand static; as the blade reaches approximately 180° on its journey you will have to turn the sword hand in to allow the point to continue circling without hitting the wall in front; you now re-join the 'path to parry 3' as the blade reaches the 270° mark (point out to the non-sword side, blade parallel to the ground); wipe up and out across the face until you reconnect with the opposing blade and again redirect to the green.

Every parry has a counter (or circular) parry move which takes the blade in a complete circle and returns it to the original parry position, necessitating a twist of the wrist on the way.

The exercise is simple – but again, 'simple' is not the same as 'easy':

1. Stand in front of a wall in the P1 position
2. Circle the blade without touching the wall through 360° back to P1
3. Move the blade to P2
4. Circle the blade back to P2
5. Move the blade to P3
6. Circle it back to P3
7. Move to P4
8. Circle to P4
9. Repeat until perfect!

Fingerwork 5 – Counter Parries

(CP2…It is not for nothing that this is known as the Actor's Parry! It's is the one we all enjoy – big, spectacular, and swashbuckling!)

There now follows an exercise which has the aggressor attacking all four lines and the defender protecting themselves with lateral and circular (a term which includes *semi*-circular) parries.

Done carefully and diligently this exercise will reveal pretty much all there is to know about basic attack and defence with swords…so take your time and understand fully both the offensive and defensive moves.

1. With a partner, stand at extending distance and have your partner extend to 1.
2. You P1
3. They disengage over to 1
4. You counter-parry 1 (Circular Parry 1 = CP1)
5. They disengage over to 2
6. You will lateral parry 2 (simply move the parry from non-sword side to sword side keeping the blade vertical and the sword hand as if it were stuck through a letterbox. Refer to the previous chapter *Fingerwork 3 – The Path of the Parry* should you need reminding about lateral parries).
7. They disengage over to 2
8. You CP2
9. They disengage to 3 (this is a semi-circular point journey from low line sword side to high line sword side – from sword hip to sword bicep.)

Fingerwork 5 – Counter Parries

10. You perform a semi-circular move into and out from the body (right handers will go clockwise and lefties anticlock) travelling the blade from low line sword side P2 to high line sword side P3.
11. They disengage under and resume an attack in 3
12. You perform the CP3
13. They disengage under and move the point to 4
14. You lateral P4
15. They disengage under and remise to 4 *(Remise: to resume an attack in the same line, for example, you extend to three, partner makes the parry of three, you disengage and bring your point back to three. Disengaging and bringing the attack back in any other line is referred to as a 'redoublement'.)*
16. You CP4
17. They disengage to 1
18. You semi-circle to P1
19. And repeat until perfect…

'Fencing' is derived from 'defence' – not 'offence'.

Anyone can poke or slash with a pointy stick, but it requires an artist to make good the parries and master the fingerwork.

ROLLS & DESCENTS 2

Hands Free Roll

For those who are very confident of their rolling ability. So confident that they are willing to remove the safety net of their own hands...

Build up by placing less and less weight on the hands as you enter the roll until you are literally tickling the floor with your fingertips. When you are ready, move your hands further to the sides until you are rolling with your arms outstretched to the sides. (Imagine just how swashbucklingly spectacular you will look when you do this with a dagger in one hand and a rapier in the other...)

Reaction Roll

The previous variations have been designed to enhance the 'cool' factor, making you look as sleek and smooth and glossy as a pedigree afghan's coat. But what if, for example, you've just been hurled to the ground in a vicious assault, leaving you bruised and battered and with the wind knocked out of you? You cannot utilise your James Bond Action Roll. For that we need the Reaction Roll...

For the purpose of the exercise...

Go back to the original forward roll.

Step forward, hands, back of neck, roll through the spine – hold it!

Rolls & Descents 2

Instead of the soles of the feet coming to land elegantly, prior to your graceful rise to a standing finish, slap them on the floor a bit. Show the ground who's the daddy. Slapping the feet on the floor, apart from creating a very pleasing, attention-grabbing sound, also has the effect of stopping the roll rather abruptly. With a little gentle practice, you will be able to tweak the timing so that the feet actually beat the buttocks to the floor. At this point, add this: as soon as the feet have stomped, sharply raise your hips into the air. At the same time clutch the small of your back with one hand, contort your face in an expression of excruciating pain and emit a voluble, apt sound effect. The audience will immediately assume that lower seven vertebrae of your spine have been smashed asunder and you will never walk again. Imagine their surprise when…

Dive Roll

A variation on the theme of forward rolls.

As your confidence grows with the smooth execution of your pain-free, smooth and gentle forward roll, you might find yourself extending the pre-roll bit to a couple of paces before you get into the placing of the hands etc.

The next stage – if you want to try it – is to allow a moment of time after the supporting foot has left the ground and before the hands have been placed on it. This is the 'Dive Roll'. Congratulations!

Rolls & Descents 2

How big and spectacular you want to make it from here, how much time you want to spend in the air before the hands reach the ground, is entirely up to you. But always work within your limitations. Only do what you know you safely can. Build up in small, manageable, unscary steps.

Eventually you may be able to clear a body lying on the floor with your dive, or a suitcase, or a table...

Two-foot take-off:
Try starting with both feet together and getting into the roll. To walk into this variation you will need to put a little hop in at the end of your approach to bring both feet together for the lift-off.

Generally you will find that a one-foot take-off will give you more length than height and a two-foot take-off more height than length.

But whatever you try, and whatever stage you try it at, remember: the roll remains the same – hands, back of the neck, and roll gently through the spine.

Top Tip: Please note that at no time have I said that you should jump, or push off your feet to launch into the dive part of the dive roll. Although, physically, this is exactly the sort of thing you will be doing, it is essential that you think and visualise the roll as being led from the top of the spine. The top of the spine is being drawn by an invisible force forwards and tucking under which causes the roll to

Rolls & Descents 2

happen. This is what happened when we looked at the forward roll without the dive bit. There is a danger that putting emphasis on the dive bit will cause you to allow the feet to lead the move, which can result in over-rotation and heavy landings. Ouch.

Unarmed 8 - Punches

Hook

You have already learnt this. Well, almost. Re-read the piece on Up & Down Slap:

"Slapper is right-handed. Slapper stands with left foot forward. Slapper raises left hand to check distance with pointing forefinger and straight arm. Forefinger should be between 10–20cm away from slappee's face.

With left foot forward, left arm is 'longer' than right as the left shoulder is in front of the right shoulder. Without moving feet or body, if the right forefinger were extended it will only reach to the left wrist – another 20cm or so short of the victim's face. So any action with the right hand will be even safer than the threatening left forefinger – PROVIDING NOTHING IS DONE TO CLOSE THE DISTANCE.

So, the feet are set – left foot forward – the threatening – left – finger is extended, the distance is safe. The next thing to happen is the slapper's right hand is raised in a clear, pre-slap position over their right shoulder.

The slapping hand is then swung in a line across the slappee's face, which will be missed by 30–40cms."

One slight amendment to the above: *"...the slapper's right hand is raised in a clear, pre-slap position over their right shoulder."* At this point the hand now balls into a fist. *"The <u>punching</u>*

hand is then swung in a line across the <u>punchee</u>'s face, which will be missed by 30–40cms."

Cock the hand so that the inside of the wrist leads the move – as if you were going to make the strike with the heel of the hand. As the fist draws level with the face, flick the fist so that the knuckles overtake the wrist. This flicking action gives the illusion of contact and cements the effect.

Note: this is *not* a copy of a real punch, rather a theatrical version. It feels a little 'camp' to do but is surprisingly effective when performed up to speed.

Jab (to the Face)

Front-on attack in which the attacker throws a straight line punch to the victim's nose.

Victim stands in a neutral on guard, attacker faces them on guard offline. Eye-contact. Attacker raises fists, momentarily 'sets' position and then thrusts the attacking fist towards the victim's nose. The attack is online and out of distance as it must stop 20 – 30cms short of the victim. The fist must immediately recoil to give the illusion of striking something and bouncing off, and also to minimise the amount of time spent at the point of cheat. The victim reacts by throwing their head backwards appropriately and bringing one or both hands up to the face. Recommended knap is First Party; second choice is Second Party; an

Unarmed 8 - Punches

outside third choice is third party. Not recommended for this move is a joint knap…

When throwing the jab, *never fully extend* the attacking arm as this will cause you to use the elbow joint to effect the recoil by jarring against itself, which will lead to pain and possible long-term damage to the joint. Rather, rely on the muscles to bounce the arm – being elastic muscles are suited to this purpose.

This is an up & down move with the attacker facing US, 1PK; it can work equally well with the attacker facing the audience with a 2PK (1PK can work but must be slick).

Most effective is using the jab while circling – so that the puncher steps in front of (DS) the punchee, only fleetingly hitting the set-up mark, throws the punch at the precise moment their body is masking the cheat from the audience and transitioning through very smoothly.

Cross

A diagonal punch travelling from the attacker's shoulder towards the recipient's opposite shoulder, passing between the combatant's heads.

Up & down: combatants are out of distance and facing square to each other, attacker is on guard neutral. Assuming a right hand punch, attacker rocks to their right, putting their weight onto their right foot and dipping sideways as they prep the punch, they then rock sideways,

Unarmed 8 - Punches

through vertical to the left, shifting weight from right foot to left as they do so. The fist travels between the two protagonists travelling from right to left from the attacker's point of view. May be 1PK or 2PK.

Profile: combatants face each other offline – that is they line up on their inside feet. Assuming a right-handed attack, the attacker stands SR of the defender on guard offline left (left foot forward) with the toes of the right foot pointing at the toes of the defender's right foot. This position aligns the inside shoulders – the fist will be travelling from SR of the defender's head, passing it on the US side, and finishing on the SL side.

To close the distance and allow the fist to travel beyond the defender, the attacker's footwork is to XFL (move the right foot across and in front of the left). Although the fist is travelling in a straight line this footwork will cause some US drift which pulls the fist *away* from the defender.

At the point of passing the defender should turn their head in reaction as if they are trying to look at the back of their shoulder. Simply turning the head in reaction causes it to move upstage and into the passing fist and knap; by trying to look at the back of the right shoulder you will instigate a downstage drift of the head. In other words, the fist/knap and the head must be *both be moving away from each other* during the move.

Unarmed 8 - Punches

The profile version must be approached with great care and thoroughly rehearsed especially if using it with a sliphand knap coming out of a left-handed lapel grip.

Uppercut

The uppercut travels vertically from low to high, targeting the point of the chin. It is worth reviewing how it works in real life first. Stand straight and relaxed; find a point on the wall opposite and look at it, staring straight ahead (as you would look into the eyes of an attacker during a fight). Place a hand flat on your chest. With your eyes looking straight ahead, the hand is invisible, being out of your peripheral vision. Start to move the hand off the chest until it becomes visible. Now look down and see how surprisingly large the gap is between your body and your hand – the edge of your peripheral vision. This blind spot is where a real uppercut is delivered and it is effective because its' delivery is invisible. So in our stage combat, theatrical version, the uppercut begins as a huge preparation wound up back, behind and above the attacker's head. From here the fist swings down, forwards and the up, passing through the line of the face.

This is an Up & Down move which can be 1, 2 or 1&2PK.

In a Joint Knap version we can, for example, use a joint claphand knap:

1. Eye-contact
2. A preps right hand for punch

Unarmed 8 - Punches

3. B preps their right hand for the knap
4. A switches eyes to B's hand – the target
5. A swings arm down and through and connects with B's hand
6. A follows through and B immediately takes their right hand to the point of supposed contact.
7. Resume eye-contact

Reasonably straightforward, however, there is one little piece of sleight-of-hand which we need to examine. It occurs at number five: B has prepped their hand to receive A's. (This hand does not need to be near the face, in fact, from a normal standing position, the right elbow should bend and only the lower part of the arm should bend in order to raise the hand to waist height and about 20cm out from the body, in front of the navel.)

Immediately prior to contact, A must flash open their hand so that the contact is palm to palm – rather than fist to palm. It is called a claphand knap, after all. The hand must instantly re-clench after contact so that the audience sees a fist at the start and the end of the move and assume that it remained a fist during the time it was obscured from their view by bodies.

It is preferable generally for the punchee to cross their body with the furthest hand to receive the knap. Using the hand that is on the same side as the punching hand can easily fall into the trap of misalignment where the punch and the knap happen in a vertical line about 20-30cms to the left (or right) of the head – a little like watching a film when the soundtrack is out of synch..

Reverse Punch

A punch using the back of the hand to lead, usually done to someone standing close behind - and slightly to one side - of the puncher. Safeties on this move are cueing systems and bodyline stops:

Physical cues: at points during a fight there may be moment when eye-contact is physically impossible either because of geography and alignment, or simply because they have a blanket wrapped over them *(as was the case when Polonius got beaten to death behind the arras in a production of Hamlet at HMP Brixton. Because it was a prison we were not allowed to bring weapons inside, so the most famous duel in literature – and the climax of one of the world's greatest plays – was done as a boxing match. The poisoned boxing glove was a resounding, if unexpected, success! Especially when Claudius was released on bail and the part was covered by one of the prison wardens. The sight of Hamlet straddling Claudius and forcing a poisoned, gloved fist into his mouth brought the house down! The Brixton Prison Hamlet was an RSC Education project on which the author served as Fight Teacher/Director. The idea of the Poisoned Boxing Glove came from the inmates and was explained thus: Laertes cuts Hamlet over the eye with a punch in the first round; his corner then surreptitiously smear the poison onto his glove in the hope that he will repeat the punch and introduce the poison into Hamlet's bloodstream; however, during the*

Unarmed 8 - Punches

second round, Hamlet evades Laertes punches and manages to land a punch which cuts open Laertes brow. Coming out for the third and final round, the pair instinctively touch gloves in a gesture of sportsmanship, thus transferring the poison onto Hamlet's. I only wish I could claim the credit for this ingenuity!)

This is when appropriate physical cues must be put in place, such as tapping or squeezing. An alternative is to use vocal cues as countdowns and/or prompts for action.

The bodyline stop is when the active weapon (hand, elbow, foot, stave, etc.) is brought to a halt when it lines up with the attacker's body, the attacker preventing it from travelling beyond – usually behind – them to maintain a safety distance and, with a little bounce, an illusion of impact.

For example, A is strangling B from behind with their left arm, so that their face is visible to the right side of A's. B uses their right thumb, hidden from view in the mechanics of the strangle, to firmly press three times into B's right shoulder. On three, B releases their right hand, preps and delivers the backhand to A's nose.

Hammerfist
The hammerfist is the base of the fist – the other end from the thumb – with which to deliver the strike. Generally used as a variation of the jab.

UNARMED 9 - BLOCKED PUNCHES 2

Parrots & Ducks

In a previous chapter we explored an exercise in which one person threw a repeated sequence of four 'punches' at four different targets – two high line, two low line - using the biceps and hips as aiming points. These moves were met by partner's counter-tactic – using their forearm to meet 'n' move the incoming assault from danger (red zone) to harmless (green zone).

As stated several times in that section, this is simply an exercise and not designed to look 'real' – nor should any attempt be made to make it look real: it is all about instilling habit and practice – physical memory – into the concept of effective blocking.

Blocking a Punch

Now we will take this further and apply the techniques learnt from this previous experiment to create the illusion of a real punch being negated by a real block.

For this, we need to employ the use of a passive assistant, namely Polly the Parrot. Polly perches pertly on the shoulder of the blocker: the puncher simply punches Polly on the beak…

Here is the sequence of events and the techniques involved: (please note that Polly only exists in the imagination of the puncher…):

Unarmed 9 - Blocked Punches 2

1. Eye-contact
2. A preps the punch by drawing back the arm in a big, heavily-telegraphed wind-up to a 'haymaker' (a wide, swinging circular punch much-loved in old Westerns). As the prep is being made – we'll say with the right arm – A now moves the eye-contact from B to Polly. It is imperative for the accuracy of this 'miss move' that the puncher visualises their target very specifically and doesn't just aim generally in the region to the side of their partner's head – there is little margin for error and the potential consequences of connection are obviously not desirable. There is also a feeling of terror and fear on the part of the recipient as they watch a huge punch being prepped while their assailant stares them in the eyes. Seeing the focus of the puncher's eyes switch from theirs to a specific point above their shoulder and to the side of their head instantly alleviates these fears and replaces them with a feeling of confidence and security. Try it!
3. B preps the block by bringing their left forearm across their body at waist height so that their left thumb touché the right side of their waist.
4. A throws the haymaker: however something magical happens midway through the punch's trajectory – the prep will take the right elbow behind the line of the puncher's body and bring the fist in line with or behind the right shoulder; as the

Unarmed 9 - Blocked Punches 2

punch is thrown and the elbow draws level with the shoulder, the punch ceases to be circular and transforms into a straight line, extending the arm and projecting the fist directly forwards and into pert Polly's pecker! The Right Hook has become a Straight Right and comes to a halt at a point in line with the defender's ear, directly above the outside of the shoulder. If nothing else happened, nothing would happen – the combatants are working in-distance, therefore to avoid any unpleasantness, they are also working off-target.

5. B may now move their left arm up in a circular motion to meet A's.

NOTE: remember the lesson about A keeping the fist thumb uppermost and the knuckles in a column and B's blocking hand facing inwards so that they cannot see the back of their hand. This to ensure that if there is any contact – there doesn't need to be, merely closeness – then the soft and gentle contact is between the soft, fleshy inner side of the puncher's forearm and flat and forgiving outer side of the blocker's – neither touching the other with either edge.

So we have the Parrot Punch. A hybrid punch designed specifically to be blocked.

Unarmed 9 - Blocked Punches 2

The timing of the move has been broken down into six beats:

Beat 1 – eye-contact
Beat 2 – move eye-contact & prep punch
Beat 3 – prep block
Beat 4 – throw punch
Beat 5 – raise block
Beat 6 – resume eye-contact

One *move* has six *parts*, which must *all* happen and all happen *in the correct order*. They must be learned in order and rehearsed as dialogue would be – a sequence of cues with one part triggering the next.

Again like dialogue, as the parts become learnt and fixed, so they will start to flow more smoothly into the next until the impression is of two actors performing one move as one, rather than two separate entities doing their own little bits of choreography while standing close to each other – to put it into other words, the combatants are constantly communicating and therefore always reacting.

Ducking a Punch

Elsewhere I mention ducking and write about not just bending the knees but touching the floor with at least one hand. Let me explain further:

The choreography calls for a right hook to be ducked. Simple..? The following is a breakdown of the sequence of events that should be in place. I will also point out the

Unarmed 9 - Blocked Punches 2

multiple safeties which should be built in to everything the combatants do to safeguard them from harm and to allow them the fullest artistic and creative freedom.

Performed up & down, the combatant can work out of distance (Safety 1). Always good to have a safety in operation before anything has even happened! Safety 2 is eye-contact; both actors are checking each other and either or both have the option to bail. Attacker preps the punch; Safety 3 is that if the defender doesn't do anything at this point, then neither does the attacker. (And even if they did, they would still be too far away to connect).

Defender ducks by pivoting to their right therefore turning their face away from the direction of the incoming attack, so Safety 4 is a damage limitation measure.

Defender leans forward from the waist whilst flexing the knees and touches the floor with their hand (either or both). Safety 5 here is that if you are touching the floor than your head must be arm's length or nearer to the floor which guarantees it to be at least an arm's length below the attack.

Safety 6: the defence used here is displacement of the target. It is essential that the attacker respects the integrity of the displacement. In other words, the attacker must imagine that the defender has NOT ducked and that their head is still where it was on the initial eye-contact. Focus remains at that now vacant space where the head was, and

Unarmed 9 - Blocked Punches 2

the punch travels harmlessly through this emptiness. The fist DOES NOT follow the head as it ducks! This can happen when the attacker keeps looking at the head as it ducks and the hand follows the sightline downwards.

Safety 7 is the resumption of eye-contact which happens after the defender has touched the floor *and remains in contact with it* and after the attacker has completed the swing of the punch. The defender must check that the move has finished while they are still touching earth in order to prevent a timing mishap…it has been known in the heat of performance for an actor to enthusiastically demonstrate how quickly they can recover and they did actually achieve recovery before the punch had reached halfway… This would have been avoided if they had simply looked first…

However, if the alignment is profile, the combatants will need to be in distance or the audience will wonder why the defender needed to duck at all. So the targeting becomes Safety 1. This loss of a safety, however, means that there will still be six safety mechanisms in operation instead of seven. This is usually sufficient to prevent mishaps. **But never take anything for granted and certainly never assume that someone will do something – look, check and see that they are doing it and that it is what you expect before doing anything yourself.**

FINGERWORK 6 – PRISE DE FER

Taking the Iron
A 'prise de fer' (French: translates as 'taking the iron'. Or 'Stealing the steel...') is an action in which the offender uses their blade to move and control the defender's, usually as a preparation for an attack.

Bind
Moving the opposing blade from high line to low line, or low line to the high line, on the same side of the body. For example: you come on guard and engage your partner's blade in three. By applying downward pressure on the blade with your fingers you can quickly and easily use your forté against their foible and move their blade to two. Whilst you were effectively parrying your partner when you were engaged with them in three – i.e. your blade was between their blade and your body – the bind puts their weapon inside yours, making you vulnerable in two. However, the element of surprise is on your side! Your opponent is briefly baffled as to your intention, and you attack their now very exposed three line.

Croisé
Were you to continue the movement mentioned above through two and pass the points between you and your partner to the line of one, then you would have executed a croisé – moving the opposing blade from high line to low line, or low line to high line, on the opposite side of the

Fingerwork 6 – Prise de Fer

body. While the bind moves a quarter of a circle and leaves you exposed (not covered or 'parried' in a guard position), because the croisé travels half a circle the move finishes with you engaged in one (or, more comfortably, seven), and protected.

So, a 90° move – bind – must be small and quick in order to get away with exposing yourself, so to speak... A 180° move – croisé – takes a fraction longer but moves from one protected position to another. 270° or three-quarters of a circle is plain madness: it takes long enough to allow your opponent to react, and finishes in a vulnerable position – allowing your opponent to react into an unprotected line...

However, because the end position is deemed safe – protected – a 360° is viable:

Envelop

The envelop, or envelopment, takes the point of the opposing weapon through a full circle and returns it to the starting position. The move occupies your foe's blade while you prepare your next attack.

Note: it is vital that your forté is used upon the foible of your partner's weapon so that their point is tucked tightly into your hilt; your 'letterbox' arm is allowed to move laterally on the croisé, but must remain fixed in place for the bind and the envelop. If your partner's point starts to slide along your blade, there is the danger of unexpected

Fingerwork 6 – Prise de Fer

loss of engagement – a loose point is a lethal point. Loss of engagement (and entry into peril) usually happens if:

1. The attacker is too loose with their sword hand, trying to do the whole movement with the whole arm instead of just the fingers, or;
2. The defender does something. Anything. The defender must allow the move to happen to them, not resist it, but not to actually do the move. Any active helping is dangerously counterproductive: the defender's sword and sword arm must remain held in place to ensure contact at all times and in the right areas.

Bind Off!

On occasion it may be appropriate to add a little flick at the end of the prise de fer in order to send the opposing blade outwards to one side or the other, so that the defender is clearly open and vulnerable. So the terms are appended with the word 'off' to designate such action – bind off, croisé off or envelop off. It is imperative that this flick is also appended to the end of the first part of the move so, for example, from on guard in three, croisé to the guard of seven, then flick the opposing blade out laterally in the low line on the non-sword side of the attacker's body.

Fingerwork 6 – Prise de Fer

Parry 5 & 5a

In addition to affecting a prise de fer from the four basic guard positions and from parries 1, 2, 3, 4, 6, 7, & 8, it is also possible to bind off from either of the two head parry positions. A 'bind' because, although the blade remains in the extra-high, head line, it is flicked sideways either to three or four (P5 goes to 3 and P5a goes to 4). So there, technically, is a change of line, on the same side of the body and the attacking blade is going through a 90° arc.

Beats

A beat is an action on the opposing blade – not technically a prise de fer, as it is not controlled from start to finish – again used to surprise, distract or open up the line of attack in the preparation.

From an engaged position, disengage by taking your blade away from your opponent's blade but *only by a few centimetres*. Immediately reverse direction to tap sharply the other blade, knocking it out to the same side, in the same line. A quick action which, obviously, your partner will 'ride', or go along with, and allow their blade to drift outwards.

Beat Parry

An active parrying technique to not merely block/deflect the incoming blade, but to ricochet it back in the direction from whence it came. Used to successfully defend against an attack and use the defence as a preparation into the riposte or counter-attack. The beat parry is more compatible with heavier blades where the heft of the weapon is more suited to continuous, flowing motion, rather than the staccato to-and-fro of lighter, quicker blades.

Heft: the heft of a weapon is how it moves in the hand; hefting a broadsword correctly means that you will be able to use it comfortably and with minimal muscular effort. Not allowing the blade to do the work and trying to 'muscle' it into different positions will quickly cause tiredness and cramping.

Glissade

Finally in this chapter I will mention another action on the opposing blade – one with which you are already familiar. A 'glissade' is a sliding of your blade along your opponent's. Usually this is used to elicit a reaction, for example, your opponent will add pressure to their blade, which means that if you suddenly disengage their blade will involuntarily fly out to the side. We met this technique briefly with the coupé in a previous chapter.

Unarmed 10 - Throws

Hip Throw

Attacker throws victim over hip to floor.

Victim stands in a neutral on guard. Attacker begins by facing them. Eye-contact. Attacker takes victim's right wrist in their left hand. Attacker places right hand on victim's left waist. Attacker now turns to their left. As they do this, they allow their right hand to slide as far around the victim's waist as possible, reaching for their right side. The attacker's left hand keeps the victim's right hand at head height, with the victim's right arm straight. The attacker moves their feet so that their right foot is outside victim's right foot and likewise their left. With the attacker's knees bent their hips should now be significantly below the victim's, pressed against the victim's thighs. At the same time, attacker leans victim forward by leading their right hand, whilst straightening their own legs. Victim should be laying, front to back, over attacker's hips. It should be possible to hold this position, release all hands and wave whilst balancing. Having practiced the move up to this point complete it by not releasing any of the hands, continue guiding victim's hand forwards and around to the left of the attacker's body, keeping both arms as straight as possible. Attacker gently rotates their torso to the left and victim allows their legs and feet to be gently catapulted around the attacker's body enabling them to get the sole of

Unarmed 10 - Throws

their feet on the floor in front of the attacker. Attacker then lowers the victim's body to the ground.

It is vital to always begin this move facing each other.

Hold wrist in a pronated left hand, that is, with the back of the hand uppermost. Having wound into position it is imperative that the two parties are as close together as possible to prevent any bumping or impact during the course of the throw. The back of the attacker's legs must push onto the front of the victim's shins: attacker's buttocks must be pressing onto victim's thighs and the attacker's lower back should be pushed into victim's stomach. Thus, as the victim is guided forwards, the move is a transfer of weight as the bodies roll together, not a drop of the victim's body onto the attacker's. During the latter stages of the throw, victim can support themselves to a certain extent with their left hand trailing across the attacker's back and the attacker supports, as fully as possible, the victim with their right arm around the victim's waist.

This is an in-the-round move – a Cowboy Classic, a high hook to the head is blocked, the arm grabbed, and in a spectacular reversal the assailant has become the victim and is on his back across the poker table…

Irish Whip

Popularised by professional wrestling, the Irish Whip apparently is a throw stemming from a desire not to have your arm twisted out of its socket by your opponent. In reality all it is a shoulder roll with your partner holding your hand!

Stand opposite your partner; if your preference is to lead your shoulder roll with your right hand, give your partner your left. Partner puts their hands around your left wrist to for a loose bracelet in which your arm is free to twist and rotate. Also to pull free through the fingers or the thumbs if you want or need to.

Partner now crosses front right and raises their arms over their head, pivoting 90° to turn their back to you. They may rise up onto their toes to help sell the move. You now take over and perform your shoulder/reaction roll. Partner follows your left arm with both of theirs, ending with a flourish.

Stomach Throw

Spectacular! Yet much simpler than it appears. It looks like your partner grabs your lapels, shoves their foot in your stomach and then falls backwards, kicking you over their heads as they go. All that really happens is that you support them to sit down and then do a forward roll!

Have your partner lie on the floor. Stand next to them at their feet. Step forward with one foot, then the other, place your hands on the ground and do a forward roll. Do it again and check that your leading foot steps roughly up level with your partner's hips, your second with their

Unarmed 10 - Throws

ribcage/armpit and your hands are placed level with or beyond your partner's shoulders. If you are both very roughly the same height this is what will happen naturally.

Next have your partner spread their feet apart where they lie. Stand between them. Take your first step up to (but not on…) their groin; take your second step and place it on the floor next to their ribs; place your hands on the floor over their shoulders and roll.

Practice this until you are both totally confident with it.

Now practice the first bit, which is a reverse Big Step Descent. Instead of stepping back into the move and sitting vertically down, extend one leg in front and sit down on the supporting leg. Do this with your partner holding your hands at first, and move onto the supporter holding the descender's wrists. Obviously we would like to give/take minimal levels of support, but practise within the realms of your own comfort.

A note on which leg to use: this depends on which foot the throwee will use to take their first step… If you are going to step forward first on your right foot, then your partner will need to extend their right foot as this will be the foot that will be tucked into your stomach. When I say tucked into your stomach, I actually mean positioned on the throwee's left hip with the toes angled outwards so as not to block the leg from moving forward on the second step. (This 'throwing' leg is merely for show, doesn't actually do anything – certainly doesn't kick the throwee overhead – and usually will naturally find its own way out of the move without the thrower having to do anything).

Once you are confidant and happy to proceed, carefully get into position; face each other; thrower places hands on throwee's shoulders (this will ultimately be a double lapel grip); throwee grasps thrower's wrists; thrower sits, supported; as soon as throwee feels that they are being pulled forwards they take step one, then step two and follow with the roll.

Practice will smooth out the move, with more work needed on the entry and some reaction acting for the end.

Body Slam
Another wrestling favourite! Basically A puts one arm between B's legs and the other over one of their shoulders, picks them up off the floor while inverting them, and drops them onto their back.

We are now in the land of rough and tumble and I include this move by way of illustration of the line between what I would and wouldn't expect an actor to attempt. While the throwee can jump into the move, brace themselves on the thrower's leg and absorb the impact by landing flat and breakfalling with arms and feet there will be an impact, therefore there will be some pain. And that is not what I would expect an actor to do. Obviously there are physical

Unarmed 10 - Throws

types out there who welcome and enjoy this level of physicality and don't mind taking the odd bruise.

But, as I say, it is not a move I would teach as a rule, and it is not one I would expect an actor to undertake.

Unarmed 11 – Profile & ITR Slaps

Profile Slap

Here is the profile version which depends on non-telegraphy, i.e. the audience are left with the thought "Gosh, A has just slapped B". In other words, it happens too fast for the eye to see.

A & B are facing each other, their profiles to the audience (profile configuration). Both A & B's hands are by their sides. A, copying the action of a Wild West quick draw ace, flicks their hand by the side of B's upstage ear, as if they had a sweet wrapper stuck on the tip of their middle finger and were trying to flick it off over their partner's upstage shoulder. Having flicked, the hand is withdrawn and should momentarily hover in the space between the two actor's heads to reinforce the image of the slap in the minds of the audience. The reaction and knap are exactly the same as in the up & down slap and, although the clap is done in full view of the audience, it happens before they are looking for it and therefore it is hidden by speed and surprise. (If the audience is looking for something after it has happened, they cannot possibly find it).

The reaction to this slap happens a fraction late. That is, not at the immediate point of supposed contact, but as the slapping hand is withdrawing: as if, in slow motion, the slapping hand has reached in, hooked the victim's ear, and pulls the head around by the ear on withdrawal. Of course,

Unarmed 11 – Profile & ITR Slaps

the ear is not touched – the hand should never get closer than a good 10cm from the victim's head.

Slap – In-The-Round

First recap the up & down and profile slaps. We have a non-contact slap for the up & down position and a non-contact slap for the profile configuration – how about in-the-round?

The answer lies in a bit of both: begin with the profile slap. As the hand is withdrawn – bear in mind that it remains at least 10cms away from the head – instead of bouncing off the head area, it is pulled at a right angle so that the palm remains facing the head and is led through the space between A & B so that sightlines at 360 degrees have been catered for, you have a non-contact slap that works for an audience seated all around you.

And if there is a safe, pain-free, non-contact way of slapping someone which works from all angles, why-oh-why would anyone ever want to slap, or be slapped, for real? Laziness..?

Remember, the audience want to remain in their disbelief-suspended state when they go to the theatre. If they see a real slap it intrudes on their 'let's pretend' psyche: instead of thinking "that *character* did or didn't deserve that", they are thinking "My God! That must have hurt that *actor*." And in scene 2, three months later, the actor in question still carries four red stripes down the side of their face…

Unarmed 11 – Profile & ITR Slaps

Theatre is a world of illusion, Stage Combat is an art of illusion, never let real life intrude…

Unarmed 12 – Kicks to the Head

Kneeling Kick to the Head

Victim is on their knees, attacker kicks them in the head, under their jaw.

The trick here is that the kick, obviously, is not into the head. Rather, it is taken with the hands. Victim kneels up with their arms at their sides. Keeping the upper arms in position next to the body (don't let the elbows raise) bring the hands up in front of you and together so that they overlap, one on top of the other, roughly in line with the base of the sternum and about 25 – 30cms out from the body.

Attacker stands in front – possibly steps in on non-kicking leg – and swings leg up using the basic kicking technique. On contact, the victim's hands both go directly to their face at the place on which they have been 'kicked', reacting as they would for the basic uppercut punch.

Victim should always use their body to mask their hands, never their head. Eye-contact, then look at the hands is the order of events for the attacker, remember, you want to be looking at the target and your partner wants to see you looking at their hands, not staring into their face as you kick towards their head.

Unarmed 12 – Kicks to the Head

Victim must ensure that their hands go straight to their face on the reaction, and not let them fly away over and above their shoulders.

This is an up & down move done most easily with the victim's back to the audience. With practice, the sequence can be smoothed so that the hands arrive just before the foot. For this to work the sequence is: first, eye-contact; next, attacker looks at the space where the hands will be; then they kick to that space. The hands arrive as the foot passes through the space, connect, and immediately transfer to the face. Done slickly, this version can work even with the victim facing the audience.

Variation: the attacker does not 'break' at the knee joint, but follows through with their kick. This gives the impression of a much heavier kick. There must still be the element of removing the 'sting' of the kick, despite the follow-through. It is particularly important to master this technique for more advanced moves.

Lying Kick to the Head

The victim is lying on their side as the attacker kicks along their body and catches them under the chin.

Victim lies on their side, propped up on one elbow. Assuming the kicker is kicking with their right foot, the victim will lie on their right side and prop themselves with their right elbow. Left arm is laid as naturally along the body as possible and the arm bent at the elbow so the hand is placed in the air 20 – 30cms in front of the

Unarmed 12 – Kicks to the Head

stomach, slightly cupped with the fingers and thumb together, thumb down, palm towards the feet.

The attacker begins at the feet end of the victim and steps forward towards the head end with their left. The right leg swings through and the foot connects with the victim's hand. The hand goes directly to the chin and victim does a variation on the uppercut reaction while the attacker allows their foot to follow through, crossing the line of the face. The right leg in this instance is the inside leg, the one nearest the victim. Swinging and following through with this technique, the inside leg will naturally swing across and in front of the kicker's body – away from the victim's head. Using the outside leg to kick will direct the foot in line and towards the face – not desirable.

First, eye-contact, then the attacker looks at the target, the hand. Then the attacker steps in and kicks. That is far and away the easy job in this move as the victim has to be very specific about their position. Legs must be as straight as possible as bent knees can catch the kicking foot. The hips must be perpendicular to the ground, the uppermost hip pushed unnaturally forward to give the maximum height of back behind which to hide the hand. If this upper hip is allowed to sag backwards even a fraction, it will expose the whole cheat. Bear in mind, you only have the width of your body at its narrowest point – and fighting against gravity – to conceal the cheat.

Unarmed 12 – Kicks to the Head

This move is up & down with the victim's back to the audience. Learnt static it is a very contrived move and demonstrates a very unnatural and even more un-theatrical position of the victim. However, imagine the victim in the last throes of a fight and a previous move has sent them prostrate to the floor, as they slowly roll themselves to get up, this sadistic kick comes crashing in *à la* Clockwork Orange…

Unarmed 13 - Contact Punches & Kicks

There are some contact techniques in the repertoire, however there deployment is extremely selective and instruction and rehearsal carefully supervised.

Generally speaking, any contact made will be to a major muscle group like the abdomen or the buttocks and not anywhere near sensitive or vulnerable areas – groin, face etc. Nor will it be made near any joints

Flickhand Jab to Stomach
Punching technique whereby the fist is held loose and at the point of supposed contact, the fingers open and the backs of them lightly slap the target, the fist immediately re-clenching.

Drag Flickhand
Rather like a backhand slap only done with a clenched fist which opens to flick the target with the back of the fingers in passing – usually horizontally, left to right (when done with the right hand).

Openhand to Stomach
Contact stomach punch similar to the flickhand, except that the contact is made with the palm of the hand. To do this the combatants must be on an Offline alignment: a right-handed punch would require the puncher to have their right foot aligned with the punchee's. Even more easily done is to be standing at right angles to the recipient,

Unarmed 13 - Contact Punches & Kicks

with the punching hand obviously on the 'open' side – i.e. the side where it will not be impeded by the punchee's body.

'Karate Chop' to Neck

This technique involves placing the supporting hand on or around the victim's shoulder, telegraphed prep of the strike with the bottom edge (blade) of the hand – the 'karate chop' – and cheating the contact by turning the striking hand palm down to lightly slap the back of the supporting hand; the hand glances off the supporting hand and returns to the 'karate chop' position. Some judicious masking, for example, chopper movies to block the sightline with their body for the instant of 'contact', immediately clearing to reveal the working hand 'still' in the chopping position.

Obviously, this technique is not limited to the neck (or indeed to a 'karate chop'); I have merely cited possibly the most common application.

Double Fist to Back/Neck

Usually performed following a knee or punch to the stomach – or any other move – which has resulted in the victim being doubled-over. Again, the actual application may be varied; it is the salient elements of the technique which need to be noted: eye-contact is unavailable and so a physical substitute is put in place. I would recommend that the attacker places their hands flat on the victims back and

Unarmed 13 - Contact Punches & Kicks

use this initial contact to ensure that both participants are on balance and in position (the attacker – standing, with better view and balance – moving to readjust, *not* pulling or pushing the victim into position). When set and still, the attacker breaks contact, forms their hands into a double-fist and taps the target very lightly with the base of the fists. The weapon is then raised and brought down onto the target, opening at the last moment to make the contact with the palms of the hands, immediately re-forming the 'double-fist' to consolidate the action.

Important points to consider:

As mentioned, the actor with the easiest job at moving should be the one to move and pull or push the other person which may result in them going off balance, stumbling or falling. It is the actor's job to 'sell' that they are moving to get a better shot.

This technique utilises a 'one-two' rhythm – beat 1=the preparatory double-fisted tap and beat 2=the blow itself; it is therefore imperative that this rhythm is set and rehearsed until ingrained and without variation so that the victim is never surprised.

The 'double-fist' – there are three options, of which only two should be attempted:

    i.   Side-by-side – in which two separate fists are pushed together so the heel of the hand, knuckles one and knuckles two are pressed into each other;

ii. Overlap – in which one fist is made and the other hand is wrapped over it, heel-to-heel and the fingertips of the overlapping hand touching the third knuckles of the fist;

iii. Interlaced – where the fingers of each hand are spread and then joined by pushing the fingers of one hand between the fingers of the other.

Of these, options i and ii are acceptable: there is a danger, however slight, that the hands may 'stick' together at the moment when they should be separating immediately prior to the contact. The recommended method of avoiding the 'sticking' is simply not to use this method of joining the hands.

There is a fourth – acceptable – variation which has the hands held palm to palm at right angles to each other with the fingers together and folded over onto the back of the other hand – rather as if you were pleading or begging. The hands then would come down onto the target and flatten, but never fully separate – the fingers of one hand would slide to overlap the fingers of the other.

Contact – as in the 'karate chop' and indeed all other contact techniques – is glancing: the hands are bounced lightly off the target with no energy being directed into the victim. And remember that any contact must be made with a major muscle group and not with the victim's bones, joints, delicate or sensitive areas.

The attacker must take care *after* the blow has landed; they must not move in any way as to impede or hamper the reaction and the victim's subsequent journey. Great care must be taken not to raise a knee on the delivery and to that end I would add in to the move that the attacker rises onto the balls of their feet for the actual contact – this positive action will prevent any accidental subconscious action which may endanger the victim.

Foot Stomp to Stomach

Victim lies on their back, arms down by their sides; a right-footed attacker stands to the victim's left side/left-footed to the right side. The attacker is going to jump from two feet to land on one foot, the other apparently 'stomping' into the victim's stomach…

If we freeze the actual moment of 'stomp': attacker should be supported on their left leg (with a right-footed stomper). Support here means that *all* of the weight is on the left. I would instruct the stomper to be leaning away from the victim, partly to ensure that all the weight was on the left and any temptation to put even a little on the right was made as difficult as possible, and also in the case of any overbalancing on the part of the stomper, their body would fall away from the victim.

Unarmed 13 - Contact Punches & Kicks

The working foot hovers just above the stomach. With practice, the attacker may be able to land with their stomping foot resting on the victim's stomach, but this must be built up to, using a football, sports bag or similar substitute.

The supporting foot will be aligned along the length of the victim's body with the toes pointing headwards and the heel pointing to the victim's feet. This is to avoid accidentally landing on the victim's arm. The working foot will be at right angles across the stomach with the toes pointing away from the attacker. The reaction involves the victim doubling-up, bringing their legs and torso together. This foot position provides the thinnest profile to react around and removes the danger of a toe jamming into the solar plexus…

As the victim reacts, they can also utilise the 'box' masking technique with their hands and arms.

The final alignment/configuration point to note is that standing to the victim's left, landing on the left and stomping with the right, the attacker and the victim are face to face. This permits eye-contact and also allows the attacker to see if they need to make any positional readjustments.

Repeated Stomps

On the initial reaction the victim takes hold of the aggressor's toe and heel in an apparently defensive action.

Unarmed 13 - Contact Punches & Kicks

Aggressor now relaxes and allows the victim to raise the aggressive foot and pull it back into their stomach. Aggressor merely acts the action.

This is a technique which is very adaptable; for example, repeated strikes from a quarterstaff, or a wrestle with a chair in which the aggressor holds the back and the victim holds the legs, pulling one of them into their own stomach.

Walking Over the Stomach

Victim is lying on their back while someone walks towards them from the side and uses their stomach as a stepping stone.

This is a simple trick of effectively hopping over the body while hovering the other foot on the stomach. Again, this should be practised using a substitute stomach until the movement is effortless and confident.

Contact Kick to the Stomach, Hands & Knees

Victim is on their hands and knees, attacker approaches from the side and kicks them in the torso.

This is a contact move, therefore it is real – the attacker is really kicking the victim's body. Safety demands that the basic stage combat kicking technique be absolutely mastered before even attempting this.

With the victim on their hands and knees, the attacker approaches from either side and swings the kick directly up

Unarmed 13 - Contact Punches & Kicks

and into the major muscle group of the victim's stomach. As well as perfect kicking technique, this also involves absolute accuracy on the part of the kicker as there is only a very small margin for error.

Victim must elongate the target area as much as possible to give as big a target as possible. Kick must land on the target with only the instep making contact. Particular care must be given to avoiding the line of the first ribs as well as the ribcage in general.

There is a valid school of thought which says that when kicking a male victim use the leg nearest their feet as the toes will naturally angle themselves away from the victim's groin and when the victim is female, use the leg nearest their head as the toes will angle themselves away from the bust.

As ever, the sequence of events must be eye-contact first, and then look at the target, then kick. Ensure that the attacker is not drifting in to the victim during or immediately after the move, and that the kicking foot is replaced on the floor as quickly as possible to regain maximum stability and reduce the time spent on one leg (and potentially off-balance) to the minimum.

This an in-the-round move...

Unarmed 14 – Head Butts & Smashes

Head Butt, Up & Down

Attacker uses their forehead to smash the bridge of the victim's nose.

Eye-contact. Attacker steps in front of victim who is standing in a neutral on guard and places one hand on their chest. (If the attacker is now on guard offline left, it would be the left hand – i.e. the same hand as leading foot, or the *nearest* hand.) As the attackers head goes back to prep the butt the eye-contact is maintained. As the butt is delivered, two things must remain in place: firstly, the eye-contact (which stops the attacker's head dropping and closing the distance) and secondly the contact hand stays on the victim's chest and the arm – although flexed – is locked so that as the attacker's body moves towards the defender during the move, the locked arm moves the victim backwards by the same amount, thus maintaining distance as well as assisting with the reaction.

As soon as the butt is delivered, the attacker's head recoils rapidly and the victim's hands go directly to their face at the point of supposed impact.

At this point – and not until this point – can eye-contact be broken.

This is an up & down move which works best with the attacker's back to the audience, unless the attacker is significantly taller than the victim in which case it should be the victim's back that is to the audience. It is done best without any telegraphy.

Reverse Head Butt, Up & Down

Attacker is standing directly in front of victim. Attacker drops head forward and then jerks it back to deliver a butt to the victim's nose, using the back of the attacker's head.

No eye-contact therefore strict and clear alternative cueing and safety measures need to be in place.

In this basic example the cueing will be done with the victim placing their hands on the attacker's shoulders.

Attacker stands on guard offline (action is moving upstage so offline is a more stable on guard). Victim steps in behind attacker, their feet copying the attackers' OG position. Victim places hands firmly on attacker's shoulders. Attacker drops head forward and then jerks head back to upright position, redirecting the line of movement from backwards to upwards, as if trying to throw top of head up into the flies. Initial reaction from victim is to throw head backwards whilst bringing hands to face. The hands should slide off the attacker's shoulders and up between head and nose as an extra layer of insulation in case the head comes too far back. Note: the hands are never to be relied upon to stop the head - the attacker must always stop their own head.

The major safety features in this move are

Unarmed 14 – Head Butts & Smashes

- The position is set
- The victim controls the cue
- The attacker stops their head in the upright position

This is an up & down move which generally works best with both parties facing the audience.

Head Butt, Profile
Attacker steps in and uses forehead to smash victim's nose.

Victim is standing in a neutral on guard position in profile. Attacker faces them. Eye-contact. Attacker now moves eyes to area of air next to victim's downstage ear, above their shoulder. Attacker steps in on downstage foot and delivers attack to air beside victim's face. Victim reacts by throwing head backwards, hands come up to face.

To make the attack more effective from the audience's POV, it should be delivered on a curving plane – i.e. the attacker's head describes a shallow semicircle moving first away from and then back in towards the victim's head. This arc should not be exaggerated, but it must be there. So the attack is moving, to some degree, in a line upstage - the reaction, however, must be directly backwards as if the attack had been delivered on a Stage Left to Right (or Right to Left) plane.

This is a profile move. Assuming this move is performed with the attacker moving to turn upstage as they deliver the blow then the best choice of knap for this move is first party body knap as it will be fully closed at the point of impact.

It can work with the attacker turning to face downstage to deliver, and a first party thigh knap on the upstage thigh might be the way forward.

Reverse Head Butt, Profile

Victim is tight behind the attacker who drops their head forward and jerks it backwards to crack victim's nose using the back of their head.

No eye-contact: therefore strict and clear alternative cueing and safety measures need to be in place.

The two parties need to get set in a position of touching proximity to each other. The cue must therefore be a clear indicator which is separate from the normal movements connected with getting into this position. In this example we will use a tap to the thigh. As it is all upper bodies getting close the thigh would not normally be touched so this makes it a good cue point in this instance.

Attacker stands in profile, on guard offline. Victim approaches from behind into a position where their chest and stomach are pressed into the attacker's back and their head is over the attacker's downstage shoulder. This head position is now set – as well as being the start position it is also the final impact position, offline, in distance with the line closed. The victim, when ready, cues the attack with a positive tap on the attacker's upstage thigh. Attacker now drops head forward and sharply brings it back to its original position, redirecting the energy upwards at the supposed point of impact. Victim reacts backwards and away – i.e. slightly downstage – from the attacker, who will now take a step forward and away from the victim using the upstage foot.

This is a profile move which works best with the attacker's head passing to the upstage side of the victim's. It works equally well on the downstage side – here it is more a blocking choice.

Standing Head Smash into Wall
Victim is standing next to and facing a wall. Attacker stands alongside, grabs their head, pulls it back and slams it into the wall.

The victim does it all. They pull their head back, throw it forwards into the wall and recoil from the impact all by themselves. The attacker stands next to them, places their hands on the victim's head and acts.

Victim stands on guard offline with the toes of one foot pressed against a wall. Attacker stands next to and facing them, at ninety degrees to the wall. Attacker places both hands on the top/back of victim's head. Victim places their hands on top of attackers – do not interlock fingers. Victim draws head backwards, as if being pulled back, and

Unarmed 14 – Head Butts & Smashes

then rapidly accelerates head towards wall. Eye-contact is with wall and stays there until after the recoil phase. As the victim's head moves forward, so their hands slip off the back of their head and form up, overlapped, in front of their face. The hands are then allowed to slap the wall – directly in front of the face and overlapped. At this point the head sharply recoils backwards and the hands come immediately off the wall and directly onto the face. Meanwhile, on feeling the victim's head about to move forwards, the attacker allows their hands to slide off the victim's head, towards, in front of and in a shallow diagonal high to low, beyond their own body, to finish on the non-victim side of themselves.

This is the ultimate victim control move in stage combat. The attacker plays no part – other than acting the aggressor – in any of the move. The attacker especially does not help, in any way, the victim's heads' journey towards the wall. The attackers hand movement should be that if they were to hold onto the victim's head, they would guide the head sideways, almost parallel to the wall.

The victim's eye-contact with the wall is vital: if the eyes were allowed to drop to the floor this would close the distance and bring the forehead/crown in distance of the target.

Unarmed 14 – Head Butts & Smashes

This is an up & down and a profile move. The profile version works with the attacker's back to the audience to close the cheat by masking the gap with their head/body.

Head Smash on Floor/Table

Taking the *Advanced Head Smash Technique against a Wall* it is possible to transpose this move into a variety of different settings.

For example, with the victim sat at a table the attacker can grab hold of their head and smash their face onto the table top.

The essential ingredients remain the same:

- Total victim control
- Attacker actively moves hands away from line of attack

The same thing can be done with the victim laying or kneeling on the floor. The technique and controls are the same however, especially with the lying variation, beware the added danger of the victim's elbows smashing into the floor.

All of the above work as up & down moves. They can also work in profile provided the attacker uses their body to close the cheat at the appropriate time.

Unarmed 14 – Head Butts & Smashes

A profile variation in which the attacker remains opposite their victim – for example, seated across the table, both in profile.

For this, the victim must have their downstage arm lying flat and extended straight out in front of the on the table top. The technique is executed by the victim using only their upstage hand while their downstage arm masks the gap. The head must come down turned slightly sideways and needs to lightly bounce off the DS arm. Eye-contact is, as always, with the target.

Headlock & Head Smash Into Wall

Attacker has victim in headlock, and then runs at a wall smashing top of victim's head into it.

First revisit 'Headlock' in the Reversal of Energy section.

No eye-contact therefore strict and clear alternative cueing and safety measures need to be in place.

From the headlock position…Attacker spots target wall.

Here the cueing system can be as complex or as simple, as overt or as telepathic as the parties are comfortable with. To demonstrate the order of events here is the sequence using physical cues.

Assuming headlock is put on attacker's left side, with their left arm around the victim's neck and also assuming that

Unarmed 14 – Head Butts & Smashes

the target is an upstage wall. Attacker gets victim into position during the course of the headlock. The two parties set, ready to run upstage – both their backs are to the audience. Attacker's right hand comes away from its position to open very clearly in front of the victim's face. On seeing this clear wave in front of their eyes, if and when the victim is ready, they tap the attacker's left forearm. Attacker then returns the right hand to the grip and both parties set off for the wall.

On arriving at the wall, several things must happen nearly all at once:

- Attacker turns upper body ninety degrees to make contact with the wall down as much of their outside side as possible (in this case the left deltoid, upper arm, buttock and outer thigh) this being their secondary braking system and primary victim protection
- Attacker puts last step in on their outside leg (in this instance, the right) to place foot on ground at bottom of wall as their primary braking system
- Attacker place outside hand (in this case, their right) over the top of victim's head as the secondary, back-up victim protection, and tertiary and strictly back-up braking system for the victim
- Victim's last pace should be with their outside leg (in this case their left) and should be used as their primary braking system

Unarmed 14 – Head Butts & Smashes

- Victim's inside shoulder should absorb the deceleration as their secondary braking system
- Victim's outside (in this case their left) hand will extend forward and present palm to the wall as their tertiary braking system and primary recoil engine.

Finally, the instant contact has been made with the wall, the attacker releases both their arms, quickly clearing them away from the victim and does not move their body from the wall until the victim has completed their initial reaction. It is only safe to start moving either when the victim has stopped moving or eye-contact has been regained.

Things to look at more closely:

The Set Up: - this move comes out of another. The point at which one move ends and the next one begins must be clearly known to both parties (despite not being obvious to an audience).

The Cueing System: - Here is an example of a three-layer cue not just the usual two-way system. The Attacker is asking the victim if they are ready, the victim confirming that they are (up till now a two-way cue) then the attacker adds the third level by confirming the confirmation. Why the extra level? First, while victim control dictates what and when anything happens to the person to whom it is happening, it is the person with the best view who has

Unarmed 14 – Head Butts & Smashes

ultimate control over whether or not the move happens. Second, when there is little or no possibility of eye-contact and two people have to move as one, this system gives a 1, 2, 3 count to help time the start of the move.

The Braking Systems: - Each party has a primary braking system which relies on them stopping themselves by redirecting forward momentum into earthwards energy dissipation; they also each have a secondary back-up system which involves braking against the wall; the victim has a tertiary system, their hand against the wall but in conjunction with this is the joint tertiary back up which is the attacker's body. With their body square on to the wall the victim's head will extend beyond the waistline and into the wall. With the attacker's body at right angles to the wall, the victim's head will be kept short of the wall. How short will depend, by and large, on the girth of their attacker, but a particularly petite attacker can help by pushing the trailing hip back, further away from the wall, to win extra space between victim's head and target.

This is an up & down and a profile move but for it to work in profile the attacker's back must be towards the audience at the point of impact in order to close the cheat.

Rehearsal Notes

Rehearsal Notes

So you have a solid foundation of moves and techniques, unarmed and single sword. You doubtless want to act out a fight scene – after all, stage combat can only exist in a context. Without three-dimensional characters in a (usually) extreme situation, with clear objectives and using physical tactics and obstacles, that is all you have – moves and techniques. And that is a huge weakness. An audience watching techniques executed outside of a context, a demonstration of stage fight tricks, are far less forgiving than an audience with suspended disbelief. The former will look for and see the tricks and cheats while the latter will want to remain in suspension and learn more of the story.

Your fight teacher or Fight Director will choreograph a fight using (and adapting) some of these moves. Fight Choreography is a whole different subject and there are many safety reasons why you should only ever put a fight together with a fully qualified and experienced professional.

The Fight Director will take on board all the Given Circumstances of the production, know and understand the motivations and strengths & limitations of the characters – as well as the strengths and limitations of the actors – combine all of these elements with moves and mix in some creativity to arrive at the choreographical choices they make.

Choreography is organic, living, just as the text of the script is in the hands of a competent actor, and both should be approached in exactly the same way. You may

Rehearsal Notes

have noticed the use of a couple of Stanislavsky-isms from the Psychological Realism textbook – quite deliberate…

Many actors fall into the trap of treating the fight scene as though it were a variety speciality act as opposed to what it is – acting. This is usually because their stage combat skills are significantly less rehearsed and practised as their voice, or walking or any of the other elements of acting which are taken for granted now but had to be learnt at one time.

There are many ways of rehearsing – and as many as possible should be tried – some dependent upon the director, some on the piece, and time constraints always feature large in fight rehearsals; however, here are some practical approaches to learning, rehearsing and performing a fight scene:

Rule of three – learn, rehearse, perform. Do not move on to the second step until you have thoroughly understood and practised the first

1. Learn: the moves, the safeties, the motivations, the precise elements that constitute the choreography – footwork, eye contact, check points, timing, cheats, alignment, masking, distraction etc. This is the First Circle of Stage Combat in which you concentrate and focus solely on yourself until you can do everything that is required, at the right time and in the correct order.

2. Rehearse: The Second Circle of Stage Combat which includes yourself and your partner. While

Rehearsal Notes

the first circle is all about learning actions, the second circle is all about letting these actions become reactions (acting is reacting). This phase should be balletic, the choreography should be danced, a common rhythm discovered and established and extraneous movement eliminated – physical equivalents of unscripted lipsmacks, "Errr's" and "Ummm's".

3. Perform: turn the dance into a fight, find the scenic truth, play the context and the moments. The Third Circle of Stage Combat: understand what the audience will see and perceive – what it looks like from the front.

When learning: choreography is usually formed of units - or bits - of moves and each unit must be studied and mined exactly as if it were text. Learn through listening, watching and doing. And after each new bit has been learnt (so that it can be walked through without thinking) then separate from each other, find your own space and *write it down in your own words*. The FD will have their own choreography, the DSM will have their 'book' version, you will have your own version and your partner theirs. Do not rely on anyone else to do this for you and copy it for you.

Then return to the floor and walk through the sequence again, then double-check your notes. Now learn the next bit. After writing it down and double-checking, go to the top and walk through the first bit and the new bit. Do not learn the first sequence, then start learning the second by running the first bit and adding a new move onto the end.

Rehearsal Notes

Then trying to run the first sequence again, plus the new move and adding a second new move. You will very quickly hit the point of not remembering the new bit by the time you have gone through the preceding stuff.

Rehearse – find a common rhythm. We all have our own natural rhythm and we also all learn different things at different speeds. It is vital – as soon as you can – that you and your partner find a shared rhythm at which to work. The easiest way to achieve this is for both players to walk through the moves in slo-mo, giving each other plenty of time to mark the safeties and check that moves are coming out of reactions – reasons and meanings…

This common rhythm can then, with familiarity through rehearsal, be increased until a performance tempo is found. This will be a pace which is a little less than 'full speed' as 'full speed' is always at the expense of the acting.

At this stage it should only be necessary to run the fight a couple of times at the Fight Call – a walk-through and then a run-through - which must happen every day before the start of the first rehearsal which will contain the fight scene, or at a dedicated time on days when the fight scene isn't being rehearsed. This Fight Call must happen in the rehearsal space, and include all the props, wherever possible. In reality, of course, fight calls can and do happen anywhere and at any time that the involved actors may be free. In these circumstances it is still possible to find value working with improvised rehearsal props. And I am a firm advocate of 'finger-fencing', especially when done as a 'T'ai Chi'-style slo-mo, whole-body experience. (As opposed to a wiggling, first-finger thumb-wrestle).

Rehearsal Notes

The routine of a Fight Call prior to the first run of the day should be established, comprising a walk-through followed by a run-through (although I hate using that term in connection with sword fights). The run-through should be at about three-quarters of the performance tempo. And in performance the combatants should only aim at performing at 90% of full potential – performance nerves and adrenalin will more than make up the extra 10%!

So we arrive at the end of this Handbook. We have looked at some of the tricks and techniques and a little of their application. We ended by taking a glance at the rehearsal process leading up to performance. But I will finish where I started – this is only a book and cannot replace a qualified stage combat instructor or Fight Director.

Ignore this advice at your peril...

Index

INDEX

1&2PK. *See* joint knap
1PK. *See* first party knap
2PK. *See* second party knap
abbreviations *159*
actor's compass *6*
advance
    footwork, *34*
alignment *8*
ankle circles
    warm-up *17*
ankle flex
    warm-up *16*
arm lock – arrest *121*
arm lock – Half Nelson
    US '*backhammer*' *121*
arm rotations
    warm-up *20*
avoidances *179*
back edge *48*
back of the blade *48*
back stretch
    warm-up *24*
backward roll
    US '*back somersault*' *146*
backward shoulder roll *148*
balance *18*
beat parry *228*
beats *228*
big step descent *144*
bind *225*
bind off *227*
bite – ever widening *198*
bite – your lips *197*
bite – your thumb *198*
blade *45*
block *60*
blocking
    knaps *176*
blocking a punch *63*
blood gutter *48*
body knap *176*
body slam *234*
bodyline stop *218*
botta segretta *176*
'box' masking technique *131*
braking systems *261*
breathing *12*

Brixton Prison Hamlet *217*
buttock and front thigh stretch
    warm-up *18*
camera right/left *8*
caveman drag *124*
centre stage *4*
checking distance *86*
choreology *See* fight notation
circle of energy *120*
circular parries *See* counter parries
claphand knap *175*
claymore *49*
closing distance *84*
contact kick to the stomach - hands & knees *249*
contact knap *176*
counter parries *202*
coupé *194*
croisé *225*
cross
    star footwork *186*
cross *213*
cross guard *46*
cueing system *260*
cup guard *47*
cup hilt *49*
curtsey method descent *143*
cutover *See* coupé
cuts *39, 95*
cutting edge, *45, 48*
dagger *170*
dagger hand, *170*
degagé *194*
dialogue of the fight *90*
directors *5*
disengage *193*
disguise
    knaps *177*
distance *83*
distraction
    knaps *177*
dive roll *208*
double edge *48*
double fist to back/neck
    aka *Rabbit Punch* *244*
down stage left *6*

Index

down stage right *6*
downstage *4*
drag flickhand *243*
ducking *181*
ducking a punch *222*
ear pull *118*
edge *45*
eighth guard *44*
elbow attack to stomach *126*
engage *193*
envelop *226*
envelopment *See* envelop
epée *47*
extending distance *86*
extension *51*
eye poke – profile *199*
eye poke – up & down *198*
eye-contact *68, 199*
    safeties *10*
eye-contact *90*
fifth guard *44*
fight call *265*
fight notation *187*
fighter's compass *184*
fighting distance, *85*
finger lock *123*
finger squeeze *117*
fingerwork *37*
first guard, *42*
first party knap, *175*
fishhook *120*
fist *129*
flat of the blade *45*
flickhand jab to stomach *243*
foible *45, 48*
foil *47*
foot stamp – ITR *196*
foot stamp – profile *196*
foot stamp – up & down *196*
foot stomp to stomach *247*
footwork, *27, 55, 158, 167, 179, 185*
forté *45, 48*
forward roll
    US *'front somersault' 139*
fourth guard *43*
fuller *48*
FX knap *176*
glass walls *15*
glissade *229*

grip *46 49*
guard
    lines of attack & defence *40*
guard
    part of the sword *46*
hair pull *110*
hammerfist *218*
hand shakes
    warm-up *20*
handle *46, 49*
hands free roll *207*
head and neck
    warm-up *22*
head butt – profile, *253*
head butt – up & down, *251*
head cuts *101*
head smash into wall, *255*
head smash onto floor/table, *257*
headlock *120*
headlock & smash into wall *258*
heel lifts
    warm-up *14*
high line *39*
high line targets, *39*
hilt *45*
hip throw *230*
hook *211*
hopping
    warm-up *20*
in distance *83*
inner thigh stretch
    warm-up *19*
inside line *39*
interlocked finger wrestle *117*
Irish whip *231*
jab *212*
joint knap *175*
karate chop to neck, *244*
kick to stomach *135*
kick to the head – kneeling *239*
kick to the head – lying *240*
kicking technique *134*
knap *156, 174, 200, 236*
knap definitions *174*
knee flex and rear thigh stretch
    warm-up *17*
knee to stomach *131*
knuckle-guard *47, 49*
knuckles *110*
lactic acid *26*

Index

lateral avoidances *182*
leading edge *45*, 48
leg lock *123*
lines of attack *39*
lines of defence *39*
low line *39*
low line targets *39*
lunge
    star footwork *186*
lunge 55
lunging distance *86*
masking
    knaps *176*
middle section, *45*, *48*
muscle pairs *16*
nipple tweak *119*
no eye-contact *252*
non-sword side *28*, *40*
noodle-arm *106*
nose pull *118*
nut *49*
octave *42*
on guard 136, 186
on guard – all-purpose
    footwork *27*
on guard neutral *168*
on guard offline *169*
on guard online
    footwork *28*
online guard position *167*
openhand to stomach *243*
opening distance *84*
opposite prompt *8*
out of distance *83*
outside line *39*
parries *39*, *59*
parrot punch, *219*
parry 1 *59*
parry 2 *59*
parry 3 *59*
parry 4 *59*
parry 5 *59*
parry 5 position, *98*
parry 5a *59*
parry 5a position, *99*
parry 6 *59*
parry 7 *60*
parry 8 *60*
pass lunge *165*
pass step *158*

path of the parry *60*
physical communication *128*
physical cues *217*
physical memory 29
point, *45*, *48*
Polly the parrot *219*
pommel *46*, *49*
positive negativity 14
prime *42*
prise de fer *225*
profile *See* alignment
prompt side *8*
pronation *31*
proscenium-arch 4
psychological realism 94
pulling & pushing *124*
punches *211*
quarte *42*
quillons, *47*, 49
quinte, *42*
rapier *47*
rassemblement *190*
reaction roll *207*
recover 57
recover forward *163*
redoublement *206*
rehearsal *262*
remise *206*
retreat
    footwork, *35*
reversal of energy *103*
reverse head butt – profile *254*
reverse head butt – up & down
    252
reverse lunge *165*
reverse punch *217*
reversing the leg *133*
ring guard *49*
RofE *See* reversal of energy
rope pull *124*
sabre *47*
safeties *9*, *106*
scabbard 28
scratch to front of face *200*
scratch to side of face *199*
second guard *43*
second party knap *175*
Secondes *42*
secret knap *176*
septime *42*

Index

sequence of events, *90*
seventh guard *44*
shortening the arm *98*
shoulder circles
    warm-up *21*
shoulder roll
    aka '*combat roll*' '*aikido roll*' etc. *141*
shoulders *46*
show & go *114*
Side Stretch
    warm-up *23*
stretch, roll down & rebuild
    warm-up *13*
sixte *42*
sixth guard *44*
slap – in-the-round *237*
slap – profile *236*
Slap – up & down *152*
slapping 150
slash *180*
slip
    star footwork *186*
sliphand knap *175*
stage left 5
stage right 4
Star footwork 185
step lunge *165*
stomach punch *128*
stomach throw *232*
strangle against a wall *122*
strangle from behind *122*
strangle, getting into *114*
strangling *103*
supination *31*
supporting leg *144*

swept hilt *49*
sword *44*
sword and dagger *169*
sword foot *28*
sword side *28*
synovial fluid *18*
tang *46, 48*
targets *52*
telegraphing
    knaps *177*
telegraphing *155*
testicle grab *119*
third guard *43*
three circles of stage combat *263*
thrusts *39*
tierce *42*
tip *45, 48*
torso twist
    warm-up *23*
transitions *113*
trip *145*
up & down *See* alignment
up stage left *6*
up stage right *6*
uppercut *215*
upstage *4*
upstaging *4*
victim control *104*
walking over the stomach *249*
warm-up *11*
warm-down
    warm-up *26*
wrist stretch
    warm-up *20*

Made in the USA
Middletown, DE
14 December 2016